What Others Are Saying About This Book:

The authors use not only text and examples of successful ventures, but a variety of charts and tests to help the reader evaluate self, topic and form, and provide the mechanics of authoring and publishing. — Library Journal

It is intelligently compiled and written and, most important of all, it is responsibly encouraging.
— Book Research Quarterly

This book is a useful tool for anyone starting out and a fine reference guide for established writers.
— Arizona Authors' Newsletter

Even if you do nothing but read the quotations at the bottom of many of the pages you will receive some entertaining advice and inspiration. — Publishers Digest

If you have never written a book, or if you have written many, this book is a valuable reference. It is a comprehensive little atlas of the book writing process, from choosing a marketable topic, to researching the topic, organizing it, and marketing it. — The Northwest Review of Books

This book is easy to read, full of valuable information that is easy to apply. — Computer Exchange Review

For those of you planning to write that book someday, Is There a Book Inside You? *is a must.*
— Press News Syndicate

The entire book has a practical, fresh, no-nonsense tone and, as always in one of Dan's books, is overflowing with information, including the valuable lists in the appendix.
— Marin Self-Publishers News

The book looks at agents and what they can do, the standard publishing houses, vanity publishers, and, of course, just plain doing it yourself. If you want to go the self-publishing route, this book is a valuable tool.
—Aviation/Space Writers Association Newsletter

Is there a book

book

inside you?

Writing Alone or with a Collaborator

Dan Poynter and Mindy Bingham

Fifth Edition

Para Publishing, Santa Barbara, California

IS THERE A BOOK INSIDE YOU?
Writing Alone or with a Collaborator

By Dan Poynter and Mindy Bingham

Published by:
Para Publishing
Post Office Box 8206
Santa Barbara, CA 93118-8206, U.S.A.

orders@ParaPublishing.com
http://www.ParaPublishing.com

Copyright © 1985, 1987, 1991, 1992, 1996, 1999 by Daniel F. Poynter & Melinda W. Bingham
First Printing 1985
Fifth Edition 1999, Completely Revised
Printed in the United States of America

Library of Congress Cataloging-in-Publication Data
Poynter, Dan.
    Is there a book inside you?: Writing Alone or with a Collaborator/
    by Dan Poynter and Mindy Bingham. 5th ed.
        p. cm.
    Includes bibliographical references and index.
    ISBN 1-56860-046-1: $14.95
    1. Authorship. 2. Authorship—Collaboration. I. Bingham, Mindy,
    1950- . II. Title.
    PN147.P66 1999   98-29872
    808'.02 – dc21   CIP

To Wendy and Cricket for your patience

ABOUT THE AUTHORS

Mindy Bingham is the author or co-author of 17 self-development and children's books. *Choices, A Teen Woman's Guide to Self-awareness and Personal Planning*, first published in 1983, has sold over a million copies so far. *Challenges*, the boys' version, was released in 1984. A teacher's guide, foreign rights and a lot of well-placed book reviews soon followed. With more ideas than time, Mindy learned how to team up with a professional researcher/developer and a professional writer to produce her phenomenally successful books. Mindy is also the 15-year director of the Girls Club of Santa Barbara. Publishing began as a mission, turned into a fund-raiser and became a going business. Now she runs her own publishing company, Academic Innovations, in Santa Barbara.

Dan Poynter fell into publishing. He spent eight years researching a labor of love. Realizing no publisher would be interested in a technical treatise on the parachute, he went directly to a printer and "self-published." The book sold, the orders poured in and he suddenly found he was a publisher himself. Since 1969, he has written and published 74 books on subjects ranging from skydiving to hang gliding to computers and publishing. In the publishing field, he is widely known for his best selling *The Self-Publishing Manual, How To Write, Print & Sell Your Own Book*. He is a frequent speaker at the Santa Barbara Writers Conference, the Maui Writers Conference and many other industry events. Dan runs his own publishing company, Para Publishing, in Santa Barbara.

Mindy and Dan were prompted to write this book because so many of their friends, noting their success, approached them for the secret. Now they are revealing to you the inside story on how to write a book, alone or with help—the good life of being a published author.

CONTENTS

FOREWORD

So you are finally getting serious! You have probably had your idea for a book for some time now. Maybe you have talked about it with family and friends, given it a title, even mentally outlined a few chapters. If you are like many frustrated authors, you may not have believed that you could actually transform your ideas to paper and profit. But now you have found this book, and you are ready to investigate how to make that transformation.

It is purely and simply the best and most comprehensive book I've ever seen for the neophyte writer.

Make yourself comfortable: Settle into a large, soft armchair, get your favorite pen and notepad for notes and prepare to enter the fascinating, frustrating, exhilarating and rewarding world of book authorship. You are about to learn more than you could ever imagine, from two well-known and successful authorities in the field of writing and publishing books.

I have known Mindy and Dan for many years and have watched them grow into fine, successful publishers. But it is because they are dedicated, enthusiastic teachers that I invite them to speak on book publishing at The Santa Barbara Writers Conference. You are in good hands.

You will find this book has four main sections. The first five chapters are intended to help you evaluate yourself and your topic. Take the time to read each chapter carefully and work through each exercise. Time invested in the beginning will pay off later.

The next three sections cover the mechanics of writing a book, book collaboration and your publishing options. The processes through which Mindy and Dan guide you build the foundation on which you can construct the actual project itself: a tangible, readable, saleable book.

He has half the deed done who has made a beginning.
— Horace

But most of all, enjoy yourself with this book. Through it you have two expert guides to help you explore the intriguing world of book authorship. Once you complete *Is There a Book Inside You?*, you will be able to decide easily how (or even whether) to approach book writing.

I envy the fresh, new journey you are about to undertake, because there are few satisfactions in life greater than holding a shiny new book in your hands and being able to say, "I wrote this book."

The Spaniards have a saying: "Every man in his life should plant a tree, fight a bull and write a book." Maybe skip the bull part, depending upon your priorities, but plant that tree soon—and, starting today, begin to write that book by reading this book!

Barnaby Conrad
Founder and Director,
Santa Barbara Writers Conference

Today's preparation determines tomorrow's achievement.

ACKNOWLEDGMENT

We have not attempted to cite in the text all the authorities and sources consulted in the preparation of this book. To do so would require more space than is available. The list would include departments of the federal government, libraries, industrial institutions and many individuals.

Information was contributed by Gordon Burgett, Alan Gadney, Peggy Glenn, John Kremer, John McHugh, Deborah Michelle Sanders and Jan Venolia.

We would like to give special thanks to the following people who collaborated with us on this book on collaboration:

Contributors
  Jim Comiskey, permission to adapt his
  self-evaluation exercises
  Heather Johnston Nicholson, manuscript ideas
  and direction
  Michele Jackman, business management exercises
Peer reviewers
  Charles Kent, Esquire, recommendations, approval of
  contracts and legal advice
  Pam Deuel, overall concepts and content
Editors for different editions
  Sandy Stryker, content editing
  Gail Kearns, content editing
  Nancy Capelle, copyediting
  Barbara Greene, copyediting
Design
  Robert Howard, cover
  Christine Nolt, Cirrus Design, book design
  and typography

We sincerely thank all these fine people, and we know they are proud of their contribution to this work.

DISCLAIMER

This book is designed to provide information in regard to the subject matter covered. It is sold with the understanding that the publisher and authors are not engaged in rendering legal, accounting or other professional services. If legal or other expert assistance is required, the services of a competent professional should be sought.

It is not the purpose of this manual to reprint all the information that is otherwise available to authors and/or publishers but to complement, amplify and supplement other texts. For more information, see the many references in the Appendix.

Book writing is not a get-rich-quick scheme. Anyone who decides to write a book must expect to invest a lot of time and effort without any guarantee of success.

Every effort has been made to make this manual as complete and as accurate as possible. However, there **may be mistakes** both typographical and in content. Therefore, this text should be used only as a general guide and not as the ultimate source of writing/publishing information. Furthermore, this manual contains information on writing/publishing only up to the printing date.

The purpose of this manual is to educate and entertain. The authors and Para Publishing shall have neither liability nor responsibility to any person or entity with respect to any loss or damage caused or alleged to be caused directly or indirectly by the information contained in this book.

If you do not wish to be bound by the above, you may return this book to the publisher for a full refund.

Books are embalmed minds. — C. N. Bovee

1

WHY YOU SHOULD WRITE A BOOK

Chances are you already know *why* you should write a book. Maybe the inspiration for your project struck all at once while you were driving the car, taking a shower, feeding the baby or digging in the garden. Or perhaps your idea developed over a period of time, as a series of incidents convinced you that a particular book needed to be written.

For Mindy Bingham, inspiration came as she stood at the front desk of the Girls Club of Santa Barbara. Mindy was touched when a single parent, struggling financially, exhausted and disillusioned, arrived to pick up her daughter. Living in poverty and feeling that she had no control over her own life, the woman had tears in her eyes as she asked Mindy, "Why didn't someone tell me what it would be like when I was growing up?"

As Mindy turned from the desk, she vowed to do something to help young women take charge of their lives—not just the teenagers in her care but as many young women as she could reach. And she knew the best vehicle for accomplishing her goal would be a book.

A book is the only immortality. — Rufus Choate

Dan Poynter's first book idea developed while he was managing a parachute loft in 1962. There were technical voids in parachute design and many misconceptions about parachute function. Dan was having a hard time getting his questions answered, so he set out to learn all he could about parachutes and skydiving. He began recording what he learned in a monthly column in Parachutist magazine.

A year and a half later, Dan realized that he was becoming an expert in the field, and that one way to help the skydivers and parachute designers was to put the answers they had been seeking in a book. The information he gathered eventually became a 592-page manual with 2,500 illustrations.

You should write a book because there is something you need to say, or you feel there is something other people need to know. Books are the carriers of ideas and information. They are the key to personal growth and increased satisfaction. Books unlock the mind. When you write a book, you become a part of the elite community that creates our culture and keeps it alive. And there are a lot of people and books in that community. According to a 1997 *Wall Street. Journal* article, "A staggering 1.3 million book titles are now in print, 140,000 of them first published in 1996 alone.

The chapters which follow will tell you how to author your book and get it into print, even if you do not have the time, temperament, talent, training or territory to be a "writer" in the traditional sense of the word.

As in many other parts of our lives today, tradition is playing a smaller role in the book business. In the past, books were luxuries available to only a few. Now they are necessities, bought and read by the millions of people who realize the importance of knowledge in a technological world

---

Just the knowledge that a good book is awaiting one at the end of a long day makes that day happier.
— Kathleen Norris

such as ours. As John Naisbitt and Patricia Aburdene said in *Megatrends 2000*, "In fewer than ten years the growth in information has only quickened." The information boom continues to accelerate, but as the authors point out, "Without a structure, a frame of reference, the vast amount of data that comes your way each day will probably whiz right by you." That's why it is important to be aware of the changes surrounding you. Some of the megatrends mentioned that are influencing our lives include a renaissance in the arts, global lifestyles and cultural nationalism, the religious revival of the new millenium, and the triumph of the individual.

For anyone interested in authoring a book, these facts point the way to many new opportunities. Packaged information is becoming increasingly specialized. More and more books are being printed in smaller and smaller quantities. The information in them is going out of date faster, but books are being produced more rapidly by computerized equipment.

In general, consumers feel pressed for time so they expect to gain knowledge through shorter and slimmer books. People want to know "how to" and "where to" and they will pay well to find out. This hunger for the written word extends to works of fiction as well. Perhaps because they do not have the time actually to get away, readers reach for a book when they want escape, adventure or romance.

IS IT WORTH THE EFFORT? While writing a book is not terribly difficult, it takes time and commitment. You have only 24 hours in each day. Time can be enjoyed, employed, invested or just dribbled away. Often it is simply lost—forever.

By investing some of that time in writing a book, you create opportunities that could change your whole life. Authoring a book may be the least expensive way of going into business for yourself. It can give you economic freedom.

The new source of power is not money in the hands of a few but information in the hands of many. —John Naisbitt in *Megatrends.*

During the writing process, producing a book may seem like anything but freedom. However, it is a trade-off. You work for the book now. It will work for you later.

Your published book can generate income for years while you are away doing something else. Someday, while you are lying on a beach or flying off to London, it will cross your mind that, "I'm getting paid for this!" You will no longer wonder if it was worth the effort.

Financial rewards are significant, but there are other payoffs for writing a successful book. Some of them are:

- The fulfillment of a dream
- The pride of ownership, the satisfaction of knowing it is yours
- The strong sense of accomplishment when you finish
- Reaching hundreds or thousands of people with your ideas
- Changing people's lives, or even the directions of institutions
- The good feeling you get whenever you get a letter from a satisfied reader
- The recognition of your peers

Most authors love the process and the outcome. They also love the pats on the head. If you were to ask them, we think they would agree that, yes, you should write a book.

Writing a book is an adventure. To begin with, it is a toy and an amusement. Then it becomes a mistress, then it becomes a master, then it becomes a tyrant. The last phase is that just as you are about to be reconciled to your servitude, you kill the monster, and fling him to the public.
— Winston Churchill

2

CAN YOU AUTHOR A BOOK?

Yes, you can author a book. Your knowledge and experiences are unlike those of anyone else in the world. No one looks at things in quite the way you do. Why not pass on this unique information by putting it in writing? If you have technical knowledge, a special skill, or just an interesting way of saying something, there are people waiting to buy your book.

Some people are natural writers, some are authors, and some are both. The writer is the person who puts the words on paper, while the author is the idea person. An author without interest or ability in writing can still produce a manuscript by teaming up with those who can provide the needed services—writing, researching, editing, typing and so on.

Not that it will be easy. Authoring a book may be the most challenging project you have ever taken on. But it offers rewards unlike those you will get in any other endeavor.

The first rule of writing is to keep things manageable and in perspective. Most people have to work for a living and therefore can spend only a short period of time each day on their book. Trying to keep the whole project in mind, they become confused and feel overwhelmed. Often, they simply give up, feeling they will never be able to complete their manuscript. There are several tricks to overcoming this hazard. Break a mammoth project down into bite-sized chunks. Never start at page one where the hill looks steepest. Find a work-method that is compatible with your temperament, time, talent, training and territory. Then concentrate on one section at a time and do a complete job on each one.

WHO AM I TO WRITE A BOOK? This question requires some self-reflection. You are qualified if you fall into one of these categories.

* **The Expert** is someone who has years of experience in a specific field. Experts are usually teachers, technicians or researchers. By teaching, we mean lecturing, training, writing, consulting and spreading the word. The expert has developed forms, hand-out materials and unique ways to describe the peculiarities of the field. The technician has spent time performing the occupation or activity in a hands-on fashion and can relate to the needs of the person who wants to get started in the field. The researcher usually has some recent information to share.

  Authoring a book may come easiest to experts because their subject is already known well to them. They have a ready market because those new to a field are eager to learn what they have to say. The expert's main problem is likely to be finding enough time for writing. They tend to be extremely busy people.

  But there are reasons to try to find the time. Writing a book in your field is a learning experience. It will make you better at what you do by forcing you to reorganize, reduce, condense and clarify what you know.

Michele Jackman and Cheri Jasinski owned their own management consulting firm. Their entertaining and informative lectures and workshops were well known and highly regarded. Because of the demand for

---

Some people dream of worthy accomplishments, while others stay awake and do them.

their expertise, they lead fast-paced, sometimes exhausting lives. By committing one of their favorite workshops to paper, Michele and Cheri were able to serve more people.

They completed the first draft of their book, *Super Unleaded: The Accountability Process for High Performance People*, by videotaping their day-long workshop, hiring a typist to transcribe the tape and then editing the hard copy for flow and understanding.

* **The Innovator** takes a well-known, published subject and adds a new dimension to it. Innovators are often experts who notice areas in their field that need improvement, clarification or a new approach.

While director of the local girls club, Mindy Bingham looked for material to help adolescent girls understand their career options and opportunities. When she tried to use the existing adult material with the teenagers, she discovered a "reality gap." They could not even understand why they needed to know about careers. They based their current life decisions on the notion that someone (a husband or the welfare system) was going to take care of them when they grew up. Mindy decided that a book was needed to dispel this myth and awaken young women to their future responsibilities. Choices, A Teen Woman's Journal for Self-awareness and Personal Planning, *a self-published work, sold over 40,000 copies its first year and has sold over a million since then, because there is nothing else like it.*

* **The Pathfinder** discovers and is fascinated by a new subject. When he or she finds there is little information

---

I never cease to be amazed at the huge number of folks who have valuable information between their ears who don't consider packaging and selling it. — Russ von Hoelscher available on the subject, this type of person will do the research and be the first to write a book on it. The pathfinder may not be an expert on the subject—yet. Through research, experimenting, interviewing and buying information, the pathfinder becomes the expert.

When Dan Poynter discovered the re-emerging sport of hang gliding, he was a novice like everyone else in the sport. There were no instructors; everyone built their own gliders and taught him or herself to fly. Being bookminded, he set off for the library and bookstore to see what information he could find. Unable to find a book on the subject, he wrote one. Hang Gliding, the Basic Handbook of Skysurfing, *has been through the press ten times, with 130,000 copies in print. There was no competition for the book for a year and a half. Because of the recognition the book brought him, he went on to be elected to the board of the U.S. Hang Gliding Association and later President of the CIVL, The International Hang Gliding Commission. He has received a number of international awards for his organizational work in the sport.*

You may discover a new subject that is terribly exciting to you. Certainly you are not yet an expert in it and cannot represent yourself as one. What you do have is the inquisitiveness of a newcomer—something the veterans often lose. As you study your topic more and more and find your answers, write them down. Soon you will become the scholar on that subject, and, with your notes, you will be one of the few people who will be able to tell the neophyte what he or she needs to know. You know what information the reader wants. And your research makes you a better practitioner.

We are drowning in information but starved for knowledge.
— John Naisbitt in *Megatrends*

Andy Andrews explains why he is an expert, in *How to Avoid Bicycle Theft*, as follows:

When Andy Andrews became a victim of bicycle theft himself, he found he was totally unprepared. To his frustration, he discovered there was no single central source of help to advise consumers in this area. Setting himself the goal of correcting the problem, Andrews spent the next several years studying and testing practical applications of certain procedures. He was able to come up with clear, easily followed directions to deal with the problem from both angles: first, the prevention of theft, and second, what to do if the bike is stolen. Andrews' first guide proved so successful it was soon recognized as the most complete, comprehensive and authoritative guide available to bicycle users.

One of the surest ways of producing a successful book is to be a pathfinder. The secret is to find a subject that has great potential, a large audience and has yet to be adequately covered.

- **The Artist or Creative Spirit** is a category that includes most poets and fiction writers. These story-telling artists enjoy sharing their creative thoughts, vivid imaginations, innermost feelings and personal experiences. The novel or poem entertains or evokes emotion. Like a sculptor, painter or musician, the creative writer is an artist.

Good fiction and poetry require a creative mind. According to Johnson O'Connor in *The Unique Individual*, only one person in four has what it takes. O'Connor says a creative writer would rate very high in the following traits:

- Creative imagination.
- Inductive reasoning. The ability to see what

The man is most original who can adapt from the greatest number of sources. — Thomas Carlyle

seemingly diverse elements have in common.
- Analytical reasoning. The ability to organize and arrange materials logically.
- Abstract visualization. The ability to see in your mind people, places and objects that do not exist, or at least are not present to you.
- Ability to write well. Having a sizeable vocabulary and good composition skills.

DO I HAVE WHAT IT TAKES TO WRITE A BOOK? If you evaluate your strengths and weaknesses, your assets and your limitations, you will arrive at a realistic plan that makes it possible to write a successful book. To evaluate whether you have what it takes, consider the following and then use the *book author self-evaluation* on the next page to make an objective judgment.

- Objectively evaluate the topic and unique message you wish to convey.
- Evaluate your organizational skills. Are you able to develop a well-structured outline for your book?
- Can you be dedicated to accuracy and detail?
  Are you prepared to devote the necessary time to researching your subject and to condensing it and transforming it in a way that will be meaningful to your readers?
- Are you committed to completing your book?
  Are you a starter/idea person or a starter/finisher? Do you have discipline?
- Do you enjoy writing? Do you have the skills to write well?
- Are you able to describe the pictures in your mind accurately?
- What are your time constraints?

THE BOOK AUTHOR SELF-EVALUATION

The following quiz will help you decide if you will be able author a book. Select the answer which best describes your feelings or talents by checking the appropriate box.

Knowledge of a Particular Topic

☑ 1. I know the topic well, and I enjoy discussing and studying it.

☐ 2. I am reasonably confident I can learn the information needed for this topic, and it appears that I will enjoy it.

☐ 3. I am not familiar with this topic, nor do I know whether I will enjoy studying it.

Work Habits

☐ 1. I always plan before I start a major project and then work my plan; people say I am well-organized.

☑ 2. I find that I am organized most of the time, but on occasion I do become distracted from my project.

☐ 3. I take things as they come and sometimes get priorities confused.

Accuracy and Detail

☐ 1. I take the time to research my work thoroughly before I begin a project, so I know I am doing it right.

☑ 2. Most of the time I have all my facts correct, with very few loose ends.

☐ 3. If I can't find a fact I am looking for, I tend to feel that it is not important anyway.

Commitment

☑ 1. I have tremendous drive and commitment and will not stop until the project is done.

☐ 2. I seem to have a higher level of perseverance when things are going well.

☐ 3. I start many projects but rarely find time to finish them.

Writing

☑ 1. I enjoy writing and feel it comes easily to me.

☐ 2. I enjoy writing but have to work hard at it.

☐ 3. Although I write when I have to, it is not something I choose to do.

Writing Experience

☐ 1. I already write professionally and feel confident in my writing talents.

☑ 2. I dabble in writing and would like to do more.

☐ 3. Writing sounds great, and I'd like to write a book, but I know I have a lot to learn about the mechanics.

Ability to Start from Scratch

☐ 1. I enjoy the challenge of building something from scratch on my own; I'm a self-starter.

☑ 2. If given basic guidelines, I can do a good job.

☐ 3. I really prefer to have the entire job laid out; then I will do it well.

Time

☒ 1. I control how I spend my time and have flexibility to work on whatever project I like.

☐ 2. Although I have commitments that take a lot of my time, I am organized enough to find time for the things I want to do.

☐ 3. I always feel stretched too thin and that my time is not my own.

Health

☒ 1. I have excellent health and feel good both physically and mentally.

☐ 2. I get sick on occasion, but it does not last long.

☐ 3. I have problems with my health; illness always seems to get in my way.

Self-confidence

☐ 1. I am very confident and know that I can handle any situation.

☒ 2. I am confident most of the time, particularly when I know the ground rules.

☐ 3. I am not in control of my destiny; other people really control my future.

Creativity

☐ 1. I enjoy finding solutions to problems and feel confident that if I think about a problem long enough, the answer will come to me. I like to look at the world from many different angles.

☒ 2. Most of the time I feel I can come up with the right answer or approach.

☐ 3. I try really hard to come up with the right solution, but sometimes it is just impossible.

Willingness to Risk Rejection

☒ 1. I am eager to try new things and expect that if I don't fail once in a while, I am being too cautious.

☐ 2. I want to succeed, but if I fail, I will accept it.

☐ 3. I want to avoid failure or rejection and will not take a risk if the project does not look like a sure thing.

Now find your score by adding up all the checked numbers. (A number one has a weight of 1, a number two scores a 2, and a three equals 3.) If your total score is between 12 and 17, you are a good candidate for book authoring. If you score between 18 and 23, you may want to acquire some new skills or re-evaluate your attitude and/or aptitude. A score of 24 or more means that you should rethink your motivation and your project.

Be honest. This short personal appraisal will help you focus on your personal attributes, and it may help you decide on taking the next major step in writing your book.

DON'T MOST AUTHORS HAVE A DEGREE IN ENGLISH OR JOURNALISM? No. Those authors who do not write well get help from editors, ghostwriters or co-authors. In fact, practically every celebrity book is ghosted, and most books are the effort of several people.

Dan Poynter, author of 74 books and over 500 magazine articles, took only the two required English courses in college.

Mindy Bingham, who graduated with a degree in animal science, took only one of the required English courses in college. She petitioned and was excused from further courses in composition.

WHAT IF I DON'T HAVE THE TIME OR SKILL TO WRITE FINISHED COPY? No problem, this book will show you how to locate and hire co-authors, editors, ghostwriters and other collaborators. And it will introduce you to some of the equipment available that saves time and makes writing easier.

YOUR AUTHOR WORK PLAN. On the following page you will find a self-evaluation tool to score yourself in the Five T's of Authoring: Temperament, Time, Talent, Training and Territory. This evaluation should help you understand if you need assistance with your project and, if so, in what areas. Use this exercise, along with those on the previous pages, to judge whether or not you want to proceed with your project.

You will want to return to this guide later, when you begin to finalize your plan.

GUIDELINES FOR AN AUTHOR WORK PLAN

Circle **yes** in Column II if the statements in Column I appl
to you. If they do not, circle **no**.

COLUMN I	COLUMN II
TEMPERAMENT	
I am detail-oriented	yes (no)
I am inquisitive	(yes) no
I am well-organized and work from a plan	(yes) no
I finish what I start	(yes) (no)
TIME	
I can spend at least 3 or 4 hours per day on my manuscript	yes (no)
I can make more money writing than I can at my current job	(yes) (no)
TALENT	
I know my topic well	(yes) no
I consider myself a creative person	(yes) no
I enjoy writing	(yes) no
TRAINING	
I am a very good writer	yes (no)
My grammar is perfect	(yes) no
I enjoy writing at the keyboard	(yes) no
TERRITORY	
I have a place to write	(yes) no

If you circled **yes** in Column II, refer to Column III. If you circled **no**, then the suggestions in Column IV may be helpful to you.

COLUMN III	COLUMN IV
If yes:	**If no, then perhaps you should:**
Do your own research & writing	Hire a research assistant and/or editor
Do your own research & writing	Work with co-authors
Do your own research & writing	Hire an editor or writing coach
Do your own research & writing	Work with collaborators
Do your own research & writing	Work with collaborators, writing partners and/or editors
Do your own research & writing	Hire collaborators, writing partners and/or editors
Do your own research & writing	Hire research assistants or find expert co-author
Do your own research & writing	Find a creative writing partner
Do your own research & writing	Collaborate with a writer
Do your own research & writing	Hire a professional writer
Do your own research & writing	Hire a professional editor
Do your own research & writing	Dictate your book and have someone else type it
Set up your office & storage facility	Rent space

O.K., SO I GET THE BOOK WRITTEN. WHAT ARE MY CHANCES OF GETTING IT PUBLISHED?

Anxiety over being accepted is common among neophytes in any field. After laboring over a manuscript for hundreds or thousands of hours, you are almost certainly going to worry about whether or not it will ever be in print. Try not to let your anxiety affect your project.

It is true that few of the large book publishers will accept unsolicited manuscripts. They buy from established writers and look at manuscripts submitted (and therefore screened) by agents.

But if you are an expert in your field or have something new to say about a topic that is currently "hot," publishers may indeed want to see your manuscript. While some trade books may be difficult to place, there are publishers who specialize in certain fields (religious books, medical books, art books, law books, etc.), and if your book falls into one of these categories, you should contact them. Textbook publishers are always looking for good teachers or knowledgeable professionals to write for them. Publishers of romance novels need many new titles each month and are eager to look at the manuscripts sent in by their dedicated readers.

And your chances of getting your book published could be 100 percent if you make the step from author to author-publisher. Both of the authors of this book are also self-publishers.

This book shows you how to approach publishers and also explains the very rewarding route of publishing yourself. Chapters Sixteen and Seventeen will help you select the best avenue for you and your manuscript.

In the future, editors won't tell us what to read: We will tell editors what we choose to read.
— John Naisbitt in *Megatrends*

YOU *CAN* DO IT. If all book authoring were left to the professional writers, much valuable information and many creative ideas would never make it into print. If you consider yourself an expert, innovator, pathfinder or artist, then you can author a book. If you are willing to put your energy into organization, research, recording factual information and the required follow-through, you are a prime candidate to be a published author.

In this book, we will show you several ways to bring out that book inside you. Only one has to be right for you. If one possibility "clicks," you are on your way.

In the following chapters, we will show you how to organize and write the material yourself. Then you will learn how to obtain some or all of the material and editorial help you need through collaboration with others. Finally, we will examine your publishing options to give you a better view of the entire book production process. By the time you finish this book, you will have a better understanding of how to get that "book inside you" out—a book to share with family, friends and the world.

Successful people are just ordinary people with an extraordinary amount of persistence and determination.

Nothing can take the place of persistence. Talent will not; nothing is more common than unsuccessful people with talent. Genius will not; unrewarded genius is almost a proverb. Education will not; the world is full of educated derelicts. Persistence and determination alone are the omnipotent. — Calvin Coolidge

3

WHY DO YOU WANT TO WRITE A BOOK?

WHAT DO YOU WANT FROM YOUR BOOK? Evaluating your motives will help you decide on your topic, your approach and even if you should carry on with your project. Authors have many different reasons for spending the countless hours necessary to produce a book-length manuscript. They may seek fame, fortune or self-actualization. They might want to help others, or record some kind of history or knowledge. You should be clear about your motives for writing a book before you begin.

- **Fame** in the traditional sense of the word conjures up thoughts of gala author parties, television talk show appearances, and whirlwind author tours. But fame can also mean being recognized in your community or in your profession. The most satisfying type of fame for many people is when their peers recognize them as being successful in their field.

  It takes lots of energy to maintain the high profile that goes along with fame. As an author of a recognized work, you will be asked to speak to groups, spend time away from your family and to give up part of your personal life. Some authors love the attention, while others begin to resent the extra demands on their time and energy.

- **Fortune.** According to *The Columbia University Study of American Authors* only 5 percent of the 2,239 writers surveyed earned over $80,000 and only 10 percent over $45,000. Of those authors surveyed who wrote for a living, only 28 percent earned $20,000 or more each year. Do not let these figures discourage you; just be realistic in your approach to authoring and about the word "fortune."

  Writing a book is an investment. After it is published, it will earn money while you are off doing something else. But how much money is it likely to earn? And how much time are you going to have to spend on it before it earns anything at all? It is important to consider these points carefully if you are writing for fortune.

  Maybe you define fortune as "just earning a livable income" from your writing. You may be writing in hopes of getting away from that nine-to-five job, in anticipation of a whole new lifestyle. Most authors have other sources of income, at least to begin with. Forty-six percent of the writers surveyed in the Columbia study had full-time jobs in another field.

  Many successful authors only write in their spare time. For them writing is recreation as well as a source of income. Writing provides a creative outlet while it supplements the family income.

  One way to make more money on your investment is to turn your book into a business by publishing yourself. Self-publishing requires a greater commitment of time and money but may earn you up to four times as much as the common royalty would. See Chapter Seventeen on self-publishing.

- **Self-actualization** is when you need to write the book because you have a mission to accomplish. Perhaps you have a strong feeling about a subject and want to make a

---

Writing is the only profession where no one considers you ridiculous if you earn no money. — Jules Renard statement. Or perhaps you dream of seeing your name on the cover of a book. Friends may have said just once too often, "You should write a book about that." Maybe you want to record your family history or leave something of yourself behind. Producing a book could be the fulfillment of a lifelong dream.

Evelyn Haertig spent 12 years on expensive, full-color definitive treatises on Antique Combs & Purses and More Beautiful Purses. *A retired high school teacher and antiques dealer, she discovered there were no authoritative works on the subjects. She and her photographer husband examined collections around the world. Now she and her books are world authorities on the subjects. Because of the great up-front (travel) costs, she has yet to make money on the project, but her books will be her legacy. They were something she had to do.*

• **Helping others.** Do you want to make life better for other people? Do you have a message or a methodology you think needs to be heard? Most authors of these kinds of books work in the helping or service professions.

A therapist or psychologist might see only 25 patients a week. With a self-help book, they can reach thousands of people. Someone with a unique method of teaching first-graders to read influences only 20 to 30 children at a time. By writing a book, a teacher can train hundreds of instructors, thereby helping thousands of children per year.

Your goal might be to encourage social change. A book can take a revolutionary thought, clarify it and package it. With a book, a person interested in social change can influence the course of lives, institutions or entire societies. Many important social movements began with the publication of a book.

What one has to do usually can be done. — Eleanor Roosevelt

Uncle Tom's Cabin *by Harriet Beecher Stowe brought attention to slavery and fueled the abolition movement.* The Feminine Mystique *by Betty Friedan, is considered the force that initiated the women's movement.* Rachel Carson's Silent Spring *sparked the environmental movement.* Ralph Nader's *book* Not Safe at Any Speed *dealt the deathblow to the Corvair.* Black Beauty *by Anna Sewell fostered the movement against cruelty to animals.* The Complete Book of Running *by Jim Fixx, helped to generate interest in the fitness revolution. Charles Dickens used books to bring attention to the plight of the lower class in Great Britain. Each of these people saw something new, important and shocking. Their writing, whether fiction or nonfiction, changed the thinking of society.*

• **Recording history, knowledge or expertise.** Until recently, books were the only way we had to pass on our knowledge, our history and our culture. Despite the advent of other media, books are still one of the best, most efficient and most economical ways to inform people of our shared past, our discoveries and our lives.

   The Library of Congress holds over 100 million volumes, each adding something to our collective pool of knowledge. Perhaps you, too, have valuable information or observations to pass on.

OTHER REASONS for writing a book might include:

• **Spending your spare time constructively.** For people who love words, writing can be an especially nice hobby. Whether you like to write poems, stories, novels, memoirs or whatever, writing can be relaxing, enlightening and, in many ways, rewarding.

The most powerful factors in the world are clear ideas in the minds of energetic men (and women) of good will.
— J. Arthur Thomson

- **Career advancement.** For many professionals and academics, publishing books and articles is a must in order to gain tenure, get promoted or be noticed.
- **Teaching tools.** Some very successful books came about because their authors needed a manual or a book for their own students or clients, or to explain their inventions. Are you frustrated by a lack of the precise book you need in your work? Write it!

Barbara Harris was the first to write a suitable cookbook on microwave cooking: She produced it for her cooking class students. Soon others heard about it and called requesting copies. More than ten years and 27 printings later, over 800,000 copies of Let's Cook Microwave *are in print.*

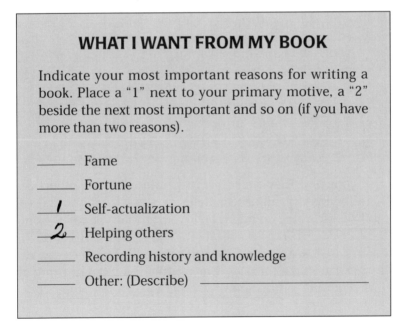

WHAT I WANT FROM MY BOOK

Indicate your most important reasons for writing a book. Place a "1" next to your primary motive, a "2" beside the next most important and so on (if you have more than two reasons).

_____ Fame

_____ Fortune

___*1*___ Self-actualization

___*2*___ Helping others

_____ Recording history and knowledge

_____ Other: (Describe) _____

It wouldn't matter if I never sold a book because my book has made my seminars and consulting possible. — Jim Comiskey

Now think, what is your primary motive for writing this book? Your secondary motive? Are they fame, fortune, self-actualization, helping others, recording history or something else?

YOUR MOTIVES FOR WRITING WILL AFFECT WHAT YOU WRITE. If you choose either fame or fortune as a top priority, you will have to write for a large market. The topic will have to be useful to hundreds of thousands of people. A well written, exciting novel is one way to meet these objectives. To achieve fame with a nonfiction book, you need to excel in a field that is currently popular: Psychology, relationship advice, health, sex, diet and finance are a few.

If you want fortune but wish to avoid fame, write under a pen name. For example, "J" wrote *The Sensuous Woman*, a bestseller. Perhaps because the subject was controversial at the time, the author was not revealed. But you can bet the royalty checks found their way to the author.

Mary P., who has a top scientific position with a major corporation, writes racy romance novels on the side. She feels she might be less effective with her all-male staff if they knew about her hobby, so she publishes under a pen name. Still, her writing enables her to pursue her other love—sports cars. Her royalty checks were recently used to buy a brand-new Porsche.

If your priorities are self-actualization, helping others or recording history, an unusually large market may not be as important to you as it might be if your primary motives were fame and/or fortune. But your work must still have a reasonably large potential audience. Publishers are in business to make money. Your motivation for authoring a book must be kept in mind when choosing your topic, but

---

I'm not trying to be taken seriously by the East Coast literary establishment. But I'm taken very seriously by the bankers.
— Judith Krantz

you must also consider your options for attracting a publisher if that is the route you want to take.

WHAT DO YOU WANT FROM YOUR FICTION OR POETRY? A priority for many fiction writers is fame and/or fortune. The fame and the fortune can grow to tremendous proportions if you become a "great American novelist." In recent years, advances of over $1 million have been paid to established writers like John Grisham, Dean Koontz, and Danielle Steel who had three novels published in 1997. Frank McCourt received a $1.25-million movie deal for his book *Angela's Ashes*. These kinds of figures are what keep thousands of hopeful novelists at their keyboards, working late into the evening. Celebrities such as Jay Leno, Marcia Clark and Colin Powell have commanded advances of several million.

Fiction can be used by the author to help others. Andrew Vachss, author of many novels (his most recent is Safe House*), is a lawyer whose only clients are children and youth. He has dedicated his life to protecting abused children and his novels are an extension of his work. Hundreds of children are safe because of Mr. Vachss and the legislation he has drafted. His first novel,* Flood*, was rejected a dozen times, then a friend of his got hold of the manuscript and showed it to someone in the publishing industry. It was finally published by Donald I. Fine, Inc., in 1985.*

Most poets write for self-actualization. And most poets do not make a living from poetry. But they feel they have something to share with others, and so they labor on.

Although you might think that recording history would be solely the work of nonfiction writers, many novelists have produced factual novels. These writers may take some literary

---

The reward of a thing well done, is to have done it.
— Ralph Waldo Emerson

liberties, but their works are helpful in understanding critical times. Herman Wouk's *The Winds of War* and *War and Remembrance* are two such books. Most events in these novels about World War II are true and the author made sure of their accuracy. And because the readers were so involved in the emotional lives of the fictional characters, many people experienced, understood and appreciated the events of the time in a much more personal way than would have been possible if they had simply read a textbook on the war. Once you have decided *why* you want to write a book, you are ready to decide *what* to write about.

Throughout this book we will make reference to other documents for more information. They are available through Para Publishing's Fax-On-Demand as well as from our Web site. Many of these reports are free. Some have a modest charge. See the Appendix for further information on how to order FOD/Web Documents.

4

WHAT KIND OF BOOK
DO YOU WANT TO WRITE?

You probably would not be reading this book if you did not have some idea of what you want to write. Before you make a final decision on your topic, take a look at some of the books being written today.

WHAT KIND OF BOOK WILL YOU WRITE? Will it be fiction (romances, children's books, westerns, mysteries) or nonfiction (how-to's, cookbooks, history, art books, travel)? Once you decide on the type of book you plan to write, check the resources in the Appendix. There you will find the titles of several books devoted to the writing and production of books on specific subjects, with more detailed information than we could possibly include here.

FICTION may be generally categorized as mysteries, suspense novels, adventures, westerns, romances, historical novels, science fiction, juveniles or young adult, children's books, Gothics and general novels. See FOD/WEB Document 606: *Publishing Fiction & Poetry* (see Appendix).

Fiction is an art and comes from emotion: nonfiction is a craft and comes from information.

- **Children's books.** With twenty million youngsters under five years of age in the U.S., there is a large market for children's books. Many couples are delaying the start of their families until they are established in their careers. Therefore they have more disposable income to spend on their children. These parents tend to be well-educated. They value books and learning and want their children to enjoy reading.

    Children's books and juveniles may be categorized as follows:

Ages 3-4 through 7-8:	Picture books
Ages 8 through 12:	Fiction and nonfiction
Ages 9 through 12:	Humorous novels
Ages 11 through 18:	Special interest books

    Children's books may be the most difficult to write. You must be accurate (children are not as forgiving as adults) and you must have a keen understanding of the children of the current generation.

    In writing for children, you have a greater responsibility, because children are less able to discriminate between good and bad ideas. For example, authors have a responsibility in their writing to be nonsexist, nonviolent and to promote self-sufficiency—particularly for girls. Fantasies should be constructive. Think back to your own childhood. Which stories are still with you—which books shaped your life?

    Illustrations provide half the charm and interest of a picture book, so most children's book writers must be artists or must collaborate with an artist. See Chapter Twelve on collaboration and the Appendix for books on how to write for children. See FOD/WEB Document 610: *Children's Books* (see Appendix).

Children's books are written to be read, adult books are written to be talked about at cocktail parties.
— Lloyd Alexander

- **Romance novels** account for 55 percent of all paperback fiction published. This fiction offers release and escape for millions of people. Readers like the action, sex and romance, and many identify with the characters. Romances are written for different audiences. Historical romances are longer stories with more adventure and historical background material, period romances concentrate on a certain historical period, and contemporary romances have a modern heroine.

  Silhouette, a well-known New York publisher, receives about 4000 manuscripts annually and publishes about 350. Approximately 50 percent of submissions are from unagented writers. Loveswept, an imprint of Bantam, publishes about 50 titles per year, five percent of the books are from first-time authors. And the romance publishers actually advertise for unknown authors. Because the romance novel conforms to a formula, it may be easier for the first-time author to write successfully.

  Silhouette reports that each of its titles sells between 250,000 and one million copies at two or three dollars per book. Royalties average between 6 and 8 percent of the wholesale price. A successful and prolific author for one of the large romance publishers can count on earning between $50,000 and $300,000 per year.

  To learn more about romance writing, see the resources in the Appendix.

- **Confessions** are classified as autobiographies or simulated autobiographies, the latter of which are fictional personal-experience stories, usually meant to inspire hope in the reader. They provide examples that readers may look to for guidance and solutions to their problems.

We romantic writers are there to make people feel and not think. A historical romance is the only kind of book where chastity really counts. — Barbara Cartland

Confession themes are simple: It takes two to ruin a marriage; if you make a sacrifice for another, happiness will come to you; you always pay for your sins. Basically, there are three types of confessions: the shocker (drugs, sex, witchcraft), the tearjerker (about the dead, dying or handicapped) and the conflict (romance, family).

• **Novels.** Novelists are the storytellers of the world. They must have a burning desire to write—as well as the time, ability and freedom to do it. Are you imaginative and good with words? Do you love to write? Are you disciplined and well organized? If so, you may have the makings of a novelist.

Fiction is entertainment and must compete for the reader's time with television, the beach and taking the kids to the zoo. A lot of fiction is written each year, but comparatively little is published. You might be more successful in selling your fiction if you consider your audience first. Stories tailored to a specific geographical area might sell well locally.

IF YOU HAVE CHOSEN TO WRITE FICTION, you should be aware that publishers in the United States receive more than 30,000 manuscripts annually, uninvited and unannounced. Of the 2,000+ novels published each year, most are written by accomplished authors. Only a few are written by unknowns or first-time authors. But, publishers are still buying first-time authors. They say the public wants fresh approaches. So it is not impossible to get your first book published. What you need are talent, tenacity and the ability to persuade a publisher or agent to read your manuscript.

Jean Auel's first novel, The Clan of the Cave Bear, *brought her an advance of $130,000 from Crown*

No wonder poets have to seem so much more business-like than businessmen—Their wares are so much harder to get rid of. — Robert Frost

Publishers, and within the first two years of production, the book had earned her over $675,000.

Once you are a known author, you can command large advances. Author Ken Follett received $12.3 million from Dell as long ago as 1990 for two novels yet to be written.

For a list of fiction publishers, see *Writer's Market.* Also see FOD/WEB Document 606: *Publishing Fiction and Poetry* (see Appendix).

Creativity in nonfiction is nice; in fiction, it is critical. You are producing entertainment and must be able to tell a story well. How you say it may be even more important than what you say.

Fiction can be more difficult to place with a publisher. The competition is very keen. But the potential for great financial reward is there. According to *The Columbia University Study of American Authors*, of 2,239 writers, genre fiction (romance, mysteries, Gothics) is the most lucrative kind of writing, with 20 percent of its authors earning over $50,000 annually from their books and stories.

POETRY is not a big seller. Even if you can sell a poem to a magazine, the payment is likely to be $20. In fact, most of the poetry magazines pay only by sending the author some free copies of the magazine. According to *The Columbia University Study of American Authors*, 55 percent of the authors earning less than $2,500 from writing were poets or those writing academically-oriented nonfiction.

Poetry, once created, must be shared and given exposure. The quantity and diversity of poetry readings and performances has grown over the last couple of decades. Poetry chapbooks, usually self-published or inexpensively published, are sold at readings. There are many prizes and

---

My books are water; those of great geniuses are wine— everybody drinks water. — Mark Twain fellowships awarded to poets. (See the current *Writer's Market* for an extensive list of contests and awards.) Attend poetry readings, mail your work off to poetry magazines and talk to other poets. Once you have received feedback from your readings and magazine exposure, you may select a grouping for publication in a book. The book should be a cohesive work with a central theme so that an audience can identify with it. Write to the American Poetry Association for a free copy of *A Poet's Guide to Getting Published* (PO Box 2279, Santa Cruz, CA 95063). *The Directory of Poetry Publishers* is $21.95 from Dustbooks, PO Box 100, Paradise, CA 95967. *Into Print: Guides to the Writing Life* is $12.95 from Poets & Writers, 72 Spring Street, New York, NY 10012, Tel: 212-226-3586.

NONFICTION does not require any great literary style. It is simply the compilation of well-researched, reorganized, updated and, most importantly, repackaged information. Of course, it is helpful if you can write well, but the content of the work is more important than the presentation of it. If you are a paint-by-the-numbers artist, you may lack the creativity for good fiction. If you opt for nonfiction and are unable to write beautifully, this book will show you how to find and work with other people who will put zip into your material.

Nonfiction books usually have a distinct purpose, which may be to inform (history, biography, exposés), to teach (how-to), to persuade (public relations), to interest and to entertain (most autobiographies, travel) and/or to inspire (arouse emotion). What counts in nonfiction is a good idea that is fresh and sharply focused—specific information on a specific topic.

The subjects with the best sales potential are how-to's, money, health, self-improvement, hobbies, sex and psychological well-being. Find a need and fill it. There are many types of nonfiction.

- **How-to's.** Most adults turn to books when they want to find out how to do something. We are a nation of do-it-yourselfers. There are how-to books on just about anything you want to learn. Most magazine articles and one-third of all books are how-to.

Jim Capossela published articles, photographs and drawings in a number of outdoor magazines. He turned out a book on sport crabbing and then wrote on how to do it in How to Write for the Outdoor Magazines. *This author, publisher and entrepreneur now operates Northeast Sportsman's Press.*

One specialized book that has been selling for years is Kershner's The Student Pilot's Flight Manual, *which has more than a million copies in print.*

Every new national craze requires factual how-to books. And, at the rate our world is changing, opportunities for writing how-to books are everywhere. Your project could be anything from a technical manual for professionals in a given field to an easy-to-follow text for anyone interested in your subject.

See the Appendix for titles of books on writing. Also check the on-line bookstores such as Amazon.com. Type in "how to write" under title search. The list that comes up is endless!

• **Self-improvement.** According to *Newsweek* there are over 1,300 books on fitness and health currently in print. Popular subjects like running are covered by many books. Some books are general, while others treat a specific aspect of the activity. Besides books on sports, there are books telling you how to eat, drink, dance, work, speak, buy, sell, play, find a job, divorce and even how to get married again.

• **Local books** are relatively easy to write and market. The

---

If you want to get rich from writing, write the sort of thing that's read by persons who move their lips when they're reading to themselves. — Don Marquis information and the distribution are local, making them an ideal project for the beginning writer and self-publisher. Tourist guides, restaurant guides and historical books are indeed an easy way to get started. The monetary success of these publications depends on the size of the geographical area and the amount of tourism. For example, in California, a book on Los Angeles might make more money than one on Bakersfield. On the other hand, competition in L.A. is likely to be keener.

Judy Dugan gathered information for a guidebook but did not know how to proceed. She worked for a typesetter and one day found herself pasting up The Self-Publishing Manual. *Armed with the answer, she approached a new bank in town about using her book as a premium. The bank bought it and she had thirty days to finish writing her book, typeset it, paste it up, print it and deliver 5,000 copies. She made the deadline and the bank gave a copy of* Santa Barbara Highlights and History *to everyone who came in during its opening week. The bank even hosted an autograph party for her. She printed 10,000 books and was on her way, selling the rest through local museums and other tourist attractions.*

• **Directories** are relatively easy to compile and are good for people who love digging up information. Your directory might cover anything from the bed and breakfast establishments in your town to a list of reviews on a certain type of book (computers, for example).

Mary June Kay published a bibliography of romance authors and titles to help readers find their favorite authors. Authors of romance novels often write under many different pen names.

John Kremer mailed questionnaires to printers and

print buyers and then assembled the information into his Directory of Short-run Book Printers.

- **Kits** are similar to directories. They are collections of all the forms and information necessary to start a business, promote a product or get listed in all the applicable directories.

Lawless J. Barrientos publishes his Starting Business Kits. *He provides blank forms, instructions, filled-in examples, lists of tax due dates and directories of important agencies. Since government forms vary, he has collections for every state. Originally, he put the kit together for his own clients. Once tested in the field, he began selling it to others. He started with direct mail advertising, sold it in office supply stores and wholesaled it to the Florida Chamber of Commerce.*

Dan Poynter collects forms and applications for book publishers and sells them in a folder as Publishing Forms. *With the kit, new publishers are able to get their books listed in all the applicable directories easily, submit them to all wholesalers quickly and register them with the proper agencies correctly. While his bestselling book* The Self-Publishing Manual *tells readers where to write for the forms, many publishers still send for the kit to save time.*

- **Cookbooks** are among the most popular of nonfiction books. Everyone eats and most people cook—there is a large market for cookbooks. Working people who do not have time for extensive cooking probably need more help with quick-to-prepare meals.

   There are four general cookbook categories: basic (general), specialty (Crockpot, chocolate, etc.), status (what the "beautiful people" are cooking) and public relations (used to promote a product or enterprise, e.g., microwave ovens).

*Rosie Daley, Oprah Winfrey's personal cook published
50 light, low-fat recipes that helped Oprah lose weight.
Entitled,* In the Kitchen with Rosie: Oprah's Favorite
Recipes, *the original hardcover edition sold more than
4.7 million copies.*

The general cookbooks are the hardest to sell because the
competition is so great. A small, easily targeted market is best
if you have a way to reach it. See FOD/WEB 613: Cook Books
(see Appendix).

• **Life stories** are often compiled by grandparents as a gift
   for their children and grandchildren. *Roots* made
   everyone conscious of their family tree and encouraged
   millions of people to conduct genealogical searches. But
   while Roots was a major bestseller, most life stories are
   self-published in small quantities for the benefit of the
   immediate family. This makes an excellent project for the
   family historian, who is sure to be immortalized as the
   person who took the time to preserve the family's
   treasured past for generations to come.

   According to Robin Hilborn, over 1,500 people are
   publishing newsletters in their own family names. With
   2.2 million Smiths in the United States, it is
   understandable that there are eight Smith newsletters.
   There are over 100,000 people in the United States
   with names such as Keller, Franklin, Jensen, Harvey,
   Weber and Ray. A book tracing your family might have
   quite a good market.

   Start by getting the Select Phone phonebook on CD,
   which has all of the telephone directories on several
   compact discs. Contact everyone with your last name for
   family history information. Once you write your family
   history, you may use this list to sell it.

• **Autobiographies.** Unless you are famous, there usually is
   not a large market for your autobiography. But if you are a
   well-known figure or associated with a famous person or
   event, making a deal with one of the large publishing

companies to publish your story could be lucrative. Katherine Graham's blockbuster autobiography *Personal History* (Knopf), which won a Pulitzter Prize, is one such example.

- **Religious and inspirational books** have always sold well and are now moving better than ever. Of course, the *Holy Bible* ranks as the number-one bestseller of all time. See FOD/WEB Document 618: *Religious Books* (see Appendix).

- **Photographic books** are usually produced by people who are photographers first and writers second. These books take many forms. They may be monographs (presenting the photographer's personal view of life), in-house books (like the Time-Life books), illustrated trade books (usually covering a single subject) or how-to books (photos are used to illustrate the text).

Andy Keech has published three volumes of Skies Call. *The full-color coffee table books, packed with unusual action shots of skydiving, contain very little writing.*

Brad Elterman published Shoot the Stars, *and tells how you can become a celebrity photographer. Sprinkled with photos of movie stars and other famous people, Brad tells how he took the shots and reveals how to break into the business.*

- **Business and professional books** are on a sharp sales increase. Business people realize it is far cheaper and faster to buy condensed, targeted information from you than to start from scratch and figure it all out for themselves. Business people can afford to invest in books and their purchases may be more impulsive, since they are spending company money, not personal funds.

    There may be more money in publishing your information in short monographs rather than in longer books. Monographs are concise booklets packed with valuable information that the average person could read in an hour or two. Timely monographs usually command a higher unit price, can be published in shorter runs and take less time to produce. But monographs must be up-to-date and filled with valuable information for a well-targeted audience to command top dollar.

• **Travel books** should be tightly focused (a golfer's guide to Kauai or the wineries of Santa Barbara County). It is not likely you can effectively compete with the large general guidebooks like Fodor's or Michelin. The best part of writing a travel book is the research—all that very deductible travel. See FOD/WEB Document 616: *Travel Books* (see Appendix).

• **History books** usually describe an interesting period or event. While they may or may not have wide appeal, they are sure to sell locally.

Mason Philip Smith spent years researching a little-known event, the Confederate raids in and around Maine, during the Civil War. His search for information led him to unpublished documents in the hands of one of the raider's descendants. He put it all in Confederates Downeast. *While many people knew of Confederate naval attacks in northern waters, few knew about the land action via Canada.*

• **Science/technical books** deal with such fields as medicine, science and engineering. Sales in this category have increased greatly in recent years. Most books have a limited professional audience, but there are exceptions. For example, Masters and Johnson's *Human Sexual Response* became a bestseller.

• **Textbooks** may sell for years and years with periodic updates or revisions. Writing a textbook now may produce returns over a long period of time. Authors of textbooks need not be recognized experts in their field when they begin writing. Many are just good teachers who see how the books currently available to them and their students could be improved. Of course, after writing a well-regarded book, they do become recognized as authorities in their field.

- **Anthologies** are collections of chapters from several different experts in the same subject area. To produce an anthology, outline the total book and decide what you want it to accomplish. Detail what you feel should be covered in each chapter. Then find experts in each area to write on those topics.

- **Republishing articles.** Many author-publishers have gone the easy route by simply editing the material of others. Deeply interested in an area, they have thoroughly researched a subject, only to find that many fine experts have already written good material on several aspects of it. The collection of these articles, one per chapter, forms a book.

  To pursue this course, contact each author for permission to use the material and ask him or her to edit a photocopy of the piece (there may be new information, or the author may want to change something). This makes your chapter better than the original article. If the chapter must be shortened, ask the author to do it. This is faster and easier than doing it yourself and then negotiating your changes with him or her.

  If, for example, you are deeply involved in the sport of skydiving, you might contact the national association and its magazine about gathering like articles that have appeared over the years and republishing them in a series of booklets. Booklet Number One might consist of all the best articles on student training. Your primary market would be the members of the association: you would sell them through the organization's "store" and via mail order by advertising in the magazine. Thus, the association is providing both the material and the customers. As the editor, you are simply repackaging the information.

  When republishing articles, do not offer royalties to

the original authors. Payments split among so many people would be small and the accounting would be overwhelming. Buy the material outright or simply offer the authors the immortality that comes from being in a book. A small honorarium and five copies of the book will be more than enough for most people.

• **Out-of-print books** may be purchased and reworked. Updating older material is usually easier than starting from scratch, and you should be able to tap the same market as the older work did. Citing the out-of-print material as the major source for your book will attract some of the original buyers.

Beverly Clark, the nation's leading wedding expert, joined forces with original author Marjorie Engel on the out-of-print book Weddings: A Family Affair. *For the revision, a new cover was designed. The original main title remained the same but the subtitle was altered. Beverly wrote the foreword for the book and updated the text to reflect the new etiquette for second marriages and couples with divorced parents.*

Bill Kaysing discovered an out-of-copyright book called Thermal Springs of the World. *He abstracted just the data on hot springs in the western United States, added some original comments and republished the work as* Great Hot Springs of the West. *Review copies sent to several major magazines resulted in an entire column of flattering coverage in* Sunset *magazine. Orders poured in and he was on his way.*

Once a book goes out of print, the rights usually revert to the author. So search out the author of the original book.

Whatever your interests or abilities, the preceding list should give you some ideas. Pick a category that appeals to you and read the next chapter before selecting a subject.

5

IS YOUR TOPIC A WINNER?

If you want to **sell** a book, not simply to write it or see it in print, you must evaluate the market size and research the competition before you make a final decision on your topic.

Once you are convinced that the subject is a good one, you are ready to choose a working title and write your back-cover copy. These exercises will give you something to hang on to, something to guide your project as you get on with the meatiest part of authoring a book.

IF YOUR CHOICE IS NONFICTION, picking a subject is your first step. You may already know what it is; you may, for example, wish to record a lifetime of experience in your field of expertise. If you come up with more than one book idea, select the easiest one with the easiest-to-reach market.

Selecting a topic is not a weekend adventure. Your book and its subject will be with you a long time. If you produce a recognized work, you will become identified with it. Think about what you want to be doing three years from now.

Whether or not you have settled on a subject, go through the following exercise.

A book is a success when people who haven't read it pretend they have.

BOOK TOPIC/AUTHOR EXPERTISE EVALUATION

Book topic: _____

Author's area of expertise: _____

To help you decide whether the book topic is right for you, write **yes** or **no** in front of the following questions:

_____ Is your information on your subject up-to-date?

_____ Do you work or participate in the field, or are you recently retired from it?

_____ Do you receive **daily** feedback on your expertise from your customers, people in the field?

_____ Do you read all the literature, attend all the conferences and continue to collect information?

_____ Do you have practical expertise as well as the required theoretical knowledge?

_____ Do people in the field recognize you for your contributions?

_____ Do you have a reputation for originality and innovation? Have you received any awards or patents in your field?

_____ Do you have the organization and discipline necessary not only to produce a book but to project the image of an authority?

_____ Are you businesslike?

If you have answered **yes** to a large percentage of the questions, you are on your way.

CONSIDER THE ELEMENTS necessary for producing successful nonfiction:

1. **The subject is interesting to you.** If you are interested in the subject, working on it will be exciting. If you are not interested, the work will be drudgery and you are not likely to do a good a job.

2. **You have the necessary expertise and the information is available.** Remember, nonfiction depends upon past experiences, research or, best of all, both. The book should be on a subject in which you are an expert or would like to become an expert. You have spent years working at, specializing in and learning something, and there are thousands of people out there willing to pay good money to get the short course on it. Write what you know!

   If you select your hobby for a book subject, there are a number of advantages: you already know what has been written, you have the contacts for gathering more information and your further participation in that hobby will become tax deductible.

3. **The subject is of interest to others and is, therefore, saleable.** Few people will purchase your autobiography unless you are already famous. Protest subjects usually have a short life and built-in audience limitations. As entertainment, fiction must compete with other media, such as television and films, which require less conscious work. All can be and have been successful books, but you must know the limitations and competitiveness of these areas.

   Anticipate reader interest and pick a subject that will sell on its own even if the buyer has never heard of you. Ask yourself "If I build it, will they come?"

How vain it is to sit down to write when you have not stood up to live. — Henry David Thoreau

4. **The subject matter is tightly focused.** We are in an age of specialization. People want information on specific subjects.

5. **The market is easy to reach.** Is the potential market so well defined that by attending a few choice conventions or by receiving reviews in a few key magazines and journals, the majority of the buyers will know about your book?

   If there are magazines on the subject, what is their circulation? If there are clubs, how many members do they have? If mailing lists are available, how large are they?

6. **The market for the subject is large enough to justify your investment of time and money.** How large is the market? Obviously the market for diet books is much larger than the one for books on repairing wicker furniture. But there are thousands of people who work with wicker furniture either professionally or as a hobby, and they may be easier to identify and reach with a targeted sales message.

   How many people should be interested, and how many can you attract to your product?
   * Identify the buyer.
   * How many people are there in this category in the United States?
   * Will all of these people buy the book? If not, how many?
   * What is the international appeal?
   * What other markets are there besides bookstores and libraries?

   For example, there are 35,000 active skydivers in the U.S. How many will buy your book on student parachutist training? Are you selling to parachuting students or skydiving instructors? How many instructors are there? Can you sell them all? Would the U.S. Parachute Association adopt your book as an instructor's resource?

Could you make money selling 500 copies a year if the price were higher and the sales went on year after year? What is the potential size of your market? Be conservative on this one. Just because you are writing a book on outboard motor overhaul does not mean that every owner of the eight million motorboats in the U.S. will buy it.

Does the topic have international appeal? Although harder to reach, what about the foreign market? But be realistic. Expanding to Canada does not double your market. The population of Canada is less than that of California and large number speaks only French.

Is there more than one market? The large publishers serve the book trade: bookstores and libraries. Fiction sells best there. Nonfiction usually sells better when you can reach the users directly. Can you sell the book by mail to a well-targeted audience? Are there hobby stores that might carry it? Can you sell it to schools or organizations? If the bookstores pick it up, so much the better. But to smaller nonfiction publishers, the bookstore sales are the frosting, not the cake.

If the market for the book is not large and you justify its creation because you just have to get it out of your system, fine. But you must realize from the beginning that this project will not be a great moneymaker. It may be reward enough to have a book to share with friends and family.

As one woman said about her self-published book on needlepoint designs of the 18th century, "I produced this book in lieu of a trip to Europe this year. The excitement I get when I fill an order outshines the good feelings I get over coffee at a bistro on the Avenue des Champs-Elysees."

The profession of book-writing makes horse racing seem like a solid, stable business. — John Steinbeck

MARKET SIZE

Circle the numbers of the statements that describe the book you are thinking of writing. To be financially successful, the book should meet at least one of the following criteria:

1. It is on a subject as yet unknown but of wide potential interest.

2. It is on a subject in which you are a recognized authority.

3. It is on a subject which will have an impact on many people in many ways.

4. It is on a subject which has not yet been covered or one where you have a fresh angle.

5. It is on a subject of recent high-level interest, a subject on which people want more current information.

6. It is on a subject that empowers people to take their life and life decisions into their own hands.

7. It covers a subject that teaches people a skill they would otherwise pay a specialist many times the cover price to perform.

WHO WILL BUY MY BOOK? WHO WILL READ MY BOOK?
Before you even sit down at the keyboard to write, you must decide who is going to buy your book. Who will need it? You must direct your writing toward a particular group of people. Be realistic. Start by defining who will be the purchaser of the book. Will it be the person who will actually read the book, or a third party such as a librarian? Or will the book be a gift item from a parent to a child? Think about the obvious purchasers and also the not so obvious.

While you might tend to focus on a topic with the largest number of possible readers, sometimes a book on a narrow topic will sell better because a lot of readers will identify with it.

Marilyn Grams, M.D., wrote a book about a breastfeeding technique she pioneered for working women. Her initial idea was to write a general book on breastfeeding incorporating her specialized information into the body of the book. This way, she felt, she would have a larger audience. But she changed her strategy and redirected the book toward the working mother. She realized that there were a number of books on breastfeeding. Her book had a unique message. And statistics show that a narrowly focused book—breastfeeding for working mothers—was really not such a narrow market as one would imagine. Over 55 percent of mothers with children under the age of one year work outside the home. Even more important, the working mother will identify more closely with this book than with a generalized breastfeeding book. Dr. Grams' Breastfeeding Success for Working Mothers is unique. Like her, find your (smaller) niche in the market.

Women provide a growing market for nonfiction books. Many women have entered the world of business. Once in the work force, they are also faced with a shortage of time. They need information and their employment provides them with the money to pay for it. Books aimed at women have great sales potential.

RESEARCH YOUR COMPETITION. If you know your field, you probably already know some of your competition. To determine whether your book subject has already been adequately covered, go to the:

I. LIBRARY

A. Ask the reference librarian for Bowker's *Books in Print,* which lists all books currently available by subject, title and author. *BIP* may be in several printed volumes or on CD. Start with the subject volumes, but also look under title and check on the people who write in this field in the author volumes. Search the *Forthcoming BIP* book for recent books. Make a list of those books you would like to review or research, or take a pocketful of coins and photocopy the pages you need. Photocopying is faster, and you will want to refer to these pages later at home. Interestingly, you will find that some of the books listed in *BIP* never went to press.

Using a red pen on your photocopies, underline the publisher (do they publish other books in this field?), the publishing date (is it an old book?) and the author (is he or she well-known in the field?).

If you find a number of similar books in your area, check the copyright dates. Old books may be out of print. Call the publishers and ask if new editions are planned. If the answer is "yes," ask how many are in print; the subject must be a good one. If it is "no," you will not have any competition.

When looking up competitive titles, check the prices. If they are all high-priced hardcover editions, you may be able to compete successfully by publishing a lower-priced softcover edition. If you find your topic has been covered extensively and recently, you need to evaluate what makes your book unique. Are you an innovator who can bring a new dimension to the subject?

B. Check the library's card catalog (on computer) to see which of the books you want to research may be obtained there. Other books may be purchased at your local bookstore or by writing directly to the publisher; addresses are listed in the back of *Books in Print.* And remember that this is probably not the only library in town. Try the local college, too; it will have different types of books.

Rate the other books as you read them:

1. Is the author an expert?
2. Is the book well-written?
3. Is the subject well-covered? (What is left out?)
4. What is unique about the book? And how can you do better?

C. Research the *Reader's Guide to Periodical Literature,* which lists magazine articles on many subjects.

D. Interview an acquisitions librarian. Ask if your proposed book would fit in with the library's collection and if the librarian would order one. Do patrons of the library ask for material on your topic?

Ask the reference librarians for help in locating material. This is their job and they love it. If you mention that you may write a book on this subject, all the better. Librarians hold authors in high esteem.

II. INTERNET

Check Amazon.com, BarnesandNoble.com and other on-line book ordering sites and systems. Do a subject search or type in a couple of key words relating to your subject and see what comes up. Most of these sites have "read more about this title" which will give you a good idea of the content of the books you see on your computer screen. You can then order any of the books you're interested in directly over the Internet.

III. BOOKSTORE

Next, visit a bookstore and:

A. Check the shelves to see what is available in the subject area you are exploring. Look everywhere; some bookstores catalog books in strange places.

   Is there another book like yours? Titles and books that appear to be like yours are usually different. In any case, you must obtain samples—to check on the competition and later for research.

B. Pitch your idea to the manager of the bookstore. Is your idea suitable for the book trade? Would it sell in a bookstore? Would the manager buy it? What types of books are people buying? A note of caution—survey at least 20 bookstores. One or two negative or glowing responses could cloud your opinion.

C. Go to your local Price Club/Costco or large discount house. Study the titles on their display tables. Here you will find in their non-fiction section the best examples of targeted titles. It seems their buyers purchase books with clear titles that convey instantly to the browser exactly what the book is about. Make a sale to one of these chains and your book has a good chance of being a bestseller.

IV. **PUBLISHERS WEEKLY**, the trade magazine of publishers, available at your library, will tell you what is coming next season. Check especially the display advertising and the *Forecast* section

V. **MARKET SURVEY**. If you still are not ready to commit your time and money to the project, try a market survey. Draft a form letter and send it to people in the field asking if they would buy the book. For example, if you are thinking about a children's cookbook, you would contact people in catalog houses and children's shops with a detailed description and ask them if there is a need and how many they would stock.

VI. WRITE AN AD. Some people place an ad in periodicals to test the saleability of a new book—before they write it.

Melvin Powers drafts and places ads for a book similar to one he is planning. If the ad pulls well, he ships the competitive book and begins writing his own. This system tests both the subject and his ad copy.

Once you have decided on your topic, you need to focus it. What will make your work special? By drafting your back-cover copy, you are forced to define precisely what you mean to say in your book. This copy will help keep you on the right path while you complete your manuscript.

VII. WRITE YOUR BACK-COVER COPY BEFORE YOU WRITE YOUR BOOK. You should be able to convey the whole idea of your book in a single sentence and describe the contents of the book in a single printed page.

Like it or not, no one reads the book before they make a buying decision. Consumers do not read it in the store. Sales reps only carry book covers and jackets to show store buyers while wholesalers and distributors say "just send us the cover copy." All buying decisions are made on the illustration/ design and the sales copy on the outside of the book. Yes, packaging is everything.

Each year, U.S. industry spends more than $50 billion on package design. Now, that is not $50 billion for the packages and certainly not for the contents. That money is for the *design* of the packages. Packages prompt buyers to reach for the product whether it be panty hose, corn flakes or hair spray.

Stores have tens of thousands of books being displayed spine-out. With all this congestion, it is hard to get attention. Initially, all buyers see is the book's spine. If they take it down, they will gaze at the cover about four seconds and then flip it over to read the back cover. On average, they will spend just seven seconds here so the trick is to keep them reading longer. Your copy has to be punchy and benefit-laden; it has to speak to the potential buyer.

Reference/Book Publishing

10th Revised Edition

Why Not Publish Yourself?

You have all the ingredients to be a successful, published author. This book is your recipe.

You will discover how easy it is to:

- **Write.** Use the easy step-by-step system for producing a commercially-successful book. Apply the simple organizational plan to research your subject and put your thoughts down on paper.

- **Publish.** Get your book into print quickly and easily by going direct and cutting out the middlemen. Copyright your own book. Set up your own publishing company and take the tax breaks.

- **Sell.** Learn the secrets of low-cost book promotion, the shocking facts about advertising and how to set up your distribution system. Find out how to promote your book with feature articles and radio/TV interviews. Then spin off electronic editions: sell your information on-line and on CD-ROM.

This manual has shown thousands of people how to break into print. You can be a published author too.

This is the first book I recommend to those considering becoming a publisher.

—Jan Nathan, Executive Director
Publishers Marketing Association

One of the best how-to-do-it books.

—Money Magazine

This is the best self-publishing manual on the market. Poynter offers more information per paragraph than many handbooks put on a page, and it's all clear and easy to follow. Highly recommended.

—Judith Appelbaum
How to Get Happily Published

Dan Poynter is the author-publisher of more than 70 books, 20 monographs, 10 audiotapes and 500 magazine articles. A consultant to the publishing field, he has coached thousands of successful publishers.

This book is your constant reference on writing, printing, publishing, marketing and distributing books. Whether you are promoting a published book or plan to write and publish one soon, you will refer to this manual again and again.

ISBN 1-56860-003-8

9 781568 600031

5 1 9 9 5 >

$19.95

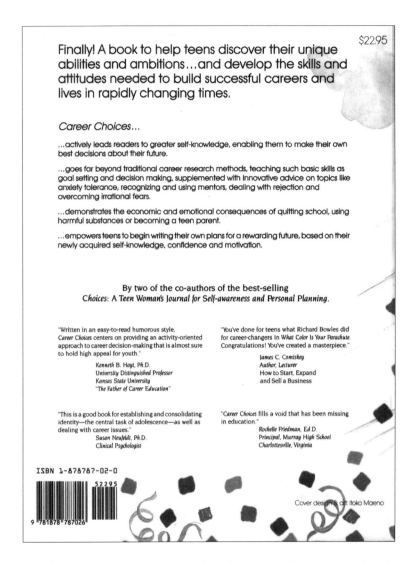

$22.95

Finally! A book to help teens discover their unique abilities and ambitions...and develop the skills and attitudes needed to build successful careers and lives in rapidly changing times.

Career Choices...

...actively leads readers to greater self-knowledge, enabling them to make their own best decisions about their future.

...goes far beyond traditional career research methods, teaching such basic skills as goal setting and decision making, supplemented with innovative advice on topics like anxiety tolerance, recognizing and using mentors, dealing with rejection and overcoming irrational fears.

...demonstrates the economic and emotional consequences of quitting school, using harmful substances or becoming a teen parent.

...empowers teens to begin writing their own plans for a rewarding future, based on their newly acquired self-knowledge, confidence and motivation.

By two of the co-authors of the best-selling
Choices: A *Teen Woman's Journal for Self-awareness and Personal Planning.*

"Written in an easy-to-read humorous style. *Career Choices* centers on providing an activity-oriented approach to career decision-making that is almost sure to hold high appeal for youth."

Kenneth B. Hoyt, Ph.D.
University Distinguished Professor
Kansas State University
"The Father of Career Education"

"You've done for teens what Richard Bowles did for career-changers in *What Color Is Your Parachute.* Congratulations! You've created a masterpiece."

James C. Comiskey
Author, Lecturer
How to Start, Expand
and Sell a Business

"This is a good book for establishing and consolidating identity—the central task of adolescence—as well as dealing with career issues."
Susan Neufeldt, Ph.D.
Clinical Psychologist

"*Career Choices* fills a void that has been missing in education."
Rochelle Friedman, Ed.D.
Principal, Murray High School
Charlottesville, Virginia

ISBN 1-878787-02-0

5 2 2 9 5

9 781878 787026

Cover design & art Itoko Maeno

Back covers of Dan Poynter's *The Self-Publishing Manual* and Mindy Bingham's *Career Choices*

Your book cover designer will lay out the package and incorporate the illustrations, put it all on disk and send it to your printer, but you must draft the sales copy. This book cover worksheet will take you step-by-step through the sales-copy draft process. Use your computer so you will be able to move the copy around once entered.

A. **Front cover.** Select a title and subtitle. Keep the title short and make the subtitle descriptive. (More on titles in a few pages.)

   List the most important person in your field (association or industry) for the foreword (and please note the spelling of *Foreword.*) You will try to get them to pen the foreword later.

B. **Spine.** Stack the **title** on the spine so it will read more easily on the shelf. Use a bold, san serif, vertical-legged typeface such as Ariel Black, bolded.

   Here are explanations for each area of the outline.

C. **Back cover.**

1. **Category.** Visit a bookstore and check the shelf where your book will be displayed. Note the categories on the books and the shelves. Listing the category on the back cover of your book will insure your book will be easy to find—because the bookshop personnel will place it on the right shelf.

2. Now you need an arresting **headline** addressed to potential buyers. You want them to relate to the book and find themselves in it. Do not repeat the title here; do not bore the potential buyer. You have already "said it" on the front. Use an alternate approach. For example, *The Self-Publishing Manual's* headline is *Why Not Publish Yourself?*

3. **Sales copy.** Concisely (two to four sentences) state what the book is about. What will the reader gain by reading this book?

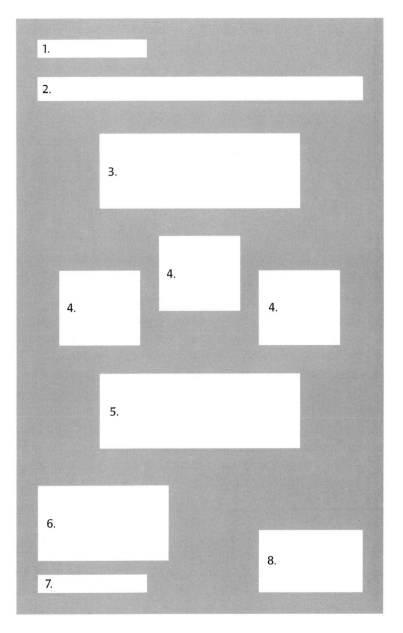

1.

2.

3.

4.

4.

4.

5.

6.

7.

8.

Back cover worksheet

Bulleted promises or benefits. Promise to make readers better at what they do. Pledge health, wealth, entertainment or a better life. Focus on who your audience is and what they want. Think about who you are talking to and what are they going to get from the book.

You will learn:

- (benefit)   • (benefit)
- (benefit)   • (benefit)

4. **Testimonials and endorsements.** Dream up three different endorsements from people you would *like* to quote. If, *This book changed my battlefield strategy.*— Colin Powell would look good, *try* it. Use *names* or *titles* recognizable in your field—sources that might impress potential buyers. This is just a draft; dress it up. You will secure some of these quotations later.

5. Show that the **author** is the ultimate authority on the subject. Just two or three sentences will do.

6. End with a **sales closer** in bold type. Ask the browser to buy the book. Use something like "This book has enabled thousands to . . . and it will show you the way too."

7. **Price.** Bookstores like a price on the book. The price is a turn-off so place it at the end of the sales copy. Never locate the price at the top of the back cover. If this is a hardcover book, place the price at the top of the front flap.

8. **Bar code** with International Standard Book Number (ISBN). The bar code on a book identifies the ISBN, which in turn identifies the publisher, title, author and edition (hardcover, etc.). Make room for, but do not worry about, the bar code and ISBN just now.

Your **title, subtitle, back-cover headline** and **benefits** may be swapped. Once you have them written down, you may wish to move some of them around. Perhaps one of your benefits would be a better subtitle.

Most back cover copy is weak and uninspiring. The title is repeated and then is followed by several quotations and a bar code and that's it! Haphazard copy is the sign of a lazy (and maybe inexperienced) copywriter. This lack of effective competition on the shelf will give you the upper hand. Book cover illustrations and design have improved tremendously over the past 15 years. Jan Nathan, Executive Director of Publishers Marketing Association, has remarked at the improved quality of the entries for the Ben Franklin Awards. Years ago, small press books tended to have unimaginative, almost generic covers. Author/publishers spent all their efforts on the text and the cover became an afterthought. Some publishers remember it was Robert Howard who brought bright, insightful, relevant, remarkable covers to the industry. There are many great cover designers today and it was Robert Howard who started it all.

If you need help with drafting mouth-watering, action-producing, customer-stampeding, riot-provoking sales copy, contact *Mr. Fire* Joe Vitale, tomorrow's copywriter at (281) 999-1110 or jgvitale@ix.netcom.com

HELP WITH SALES COPY

Years ago, we said "Write your ad before you write your book." This was to help you focus on who you were writing to and what you were going to give them. Then we realized the most important ad you will ever write is your back cover copy. Now we say: "Write your cover copy before you write your book."

Packages sell products and covers sell books. Give your books the opportunity in the marketplace they deserve. Package your text to quickly tell the idle browser what is inside.

WHAT SHOULD I TITLE MY BOOK? Start with a descriptive working title. You may change the title many times before the book is done, but you want to select something now. Early selection gives you plenty of time to live with the title, to try it out on others. Often we are so close to our title that we fail to see it is not descriptive.

The purpose of your title is to grab the attention of the bookstore browser, clearly indicate the subject of the book, create interest and target the coverage. A title should:

1. Grab the attention of the bookstore browser
2. Clearly indicate the subject of the book
3. Limit the scope of the coverage

A good title can sell 15 percent more books. A poor title may "lose" the book and keep it from reaching its intended audience.

- **Same key word as subject** Check *Books in Print.* (You did save those photocopies or printouts from the library, didn't you?) If possible, the first word of the title should be the same as the subject to make the book easy to find. The book will be listed in *BIP* by title, author and subject. If the title and subject are the same, you have doubled your exposure. Most other directories list only titles in alphabetical order; position your book where it can be found.

  COMPUTER SELECTION GUIDE, Choosing the Right Hardware & Software: Business-Professional-Personal is listed under the most common heading, "computers," while the rest of the title and subtitle tell what the book is about.

  Dan Poynter's parachuting titles all begin with the same key (subject) word:

  Parachuting, The Skydiver's Handbook
  Parachuting Manual with Log
  Parachuting Instructor/Examiner Course
  Parachuting Manual for Square/Tandem
     Equipment
  Parachute Rigging Course
  (The) Parachute Manual

Remember that computer searches are made on "key" words. Directories do not count "the" as a word in the alphabetical listings. A book entitled "Introduction to Parachuting" would be found under "I" in most directories.

- **Grab attention and make a promise.** Good book titles are the best teaser copy in both a magazine ad and on the bookstore shelf.

  Some words grab more attention than others. Hong Kong, Singapore or Haiti suggest foreign intrigue. Casino, yacht and diamonds suggest wealth. Can you think of words to suggest mystery, laughter, romance, fantasy, violence? What do these words suggest: ravish, cuddle, beauty, scar, tickle? Which title would sell more books: "Three Days" or "Three Nights"? It is amazing what image you can produce with a few words.

  Many books are sold by mail. To be marketed, they must be promoted. Here the title must grab the attention of the reader and be descriptive enough so the consumer does not need to look at the book before deciding to purchase it.

  Think about your title and come up with a good "one-liner" which tells a complete and compelling story. Spend as much time and effort as you would selecting a name for your firstborn child. The title is the single most important piece of promotional copy you will write for your book.

- **Scope.** Is your book a guide, complete, a treatise, new, a manual or a handbook?

- **Character.** Is this an academic work, technical volume, popular book?

- **Image.** Does the title project an image making the book magnetic or repulsive?

Drinking and Driving Is No Accident, How to Avoid Becoming a Victim *were the title and subtitle of Robert Penkivich's book. The problem is that while everyone is against accidents and no one wants to be a victim, the subject is unpleasant. With that subtitle, few people would read the book or even buy it. So Bob changed* the title to Drinking and Driving Is No Accident, The Inside Story. *The book is the same; only the title is different.*

• **Do not mislead.** Did you know *What Color is Your Parachute?* is about how to find a job? If you work in personnel, you are familiar with the term "golden parachute"; if you don't, you are not. Was the film *Chariots of Fire* about running in the Olympics or the burning of Rome? Is *Whack on the Side of the Head* a humor book or is von Oech trying to change your way of thinking?

Fiction titles may sometimes be cute or clever; nonfiction titles have to be descriptive. Clearly indicate the subject of your book.

Use a dictionary and a thesaurus. Avoid large words and fuzzy definitions. Try the titles out on friends. Do they know what the book is about?

The words should be easy to remember and easy to say—they should relate well to each other. A short title is best because it is easiest for a customer to remember.

Titles must read well and be grammatically correct. Do not use abbreviations or symbols/words such as H_2O that cannot be easily read. For hydrochloric acid, would you look for the book under "hyd" or "HCL"? If people are confused by a title, they will not ask for it.

• **Title length.** The title should have in it the fewest possible words that adequately describe the contents of the book. Make the title short, clear, current, specific, familiar, colorful and catchy: one to six words.

THE SUBTITLE should be longer and provide more description. If possible, your subtitle should make a promise to the reader. For example, *Sober . . . and Staying that Way: The Missing Link in the Cure for Alcoholism* by Susan Powter promises the reader the missing link to getting sober that will work for millions of people. Since *Books in Print* and most other book directories do not describe the books, your title and subtitle must do the job.

There isn't any limit to the length of subtitles, but if yours is too long, it may be abbreviated in the listings. Most listings are computerized today, and the programs only allocate so many characters to book titles/subtitles.

A WORKING TITLE gives you a name to call the book while you are preparing it. Many people get in the habit of just calling their manuscript "the book." Psychologically, a working title makes the manuscript seem much more alive.

Mindy Bingham had a bestseller in Choices, a Teen Woman's Journal for Self-awareness and Personal Planning, *but the schools needed a companion boys' edition. The working title for the new book began as* Son of Choices, *then* Choices II *or* Choices Too *and later* Changes. *Only after considerable market testing revealed that men reacted negatively to "changes' did she come up with* Challenges.

Do not get hung up on the title if it just does not come to you right away. Although many books are started with a great title (like this one. . . we constantly had people coming up to us at parties to tell us about "the book inside them" and asking for advice on how to write a book), most authors do not settle on a final title until the manuscript is nearly completed.

COPYRIGHT. While the text of books can be copyrighted, the title cannot. There are just too many books and not enough words. Check *Books in Print* and find a combination of words which does not compete with another recent book. Use generic rather than proprietary names, which may be trademarked.

NEXT make up a list of possible titles and try them on your friends and associates. Show them a title and ask them what they think the book is about. How do they react? Do they perk up? Record reactions. Big corporations spend lots of money testing names for new products. Make sure your friends are being objective and not agreeing with you just to be nice. A good title is one that gives you that "yeah!" feeling. A good title is one that sells the book.

Give me a condor's quill! Give me Vesuvius' crater for an inkstand! . . . To produce a mighty book, you must choose a mighty theme. — Herman Melville

6

WHAT WILL YOUR BOOK LOOK LIKE?

YOUR NOTEBOOK. To help you visualize your book and make your manuscript portable, lay it out in a binder. This is like framing a house before adding the interior decoration. The finishing work will be easier and more fun once you can see where you are going. Find a three-ring binder and place a label on the cover with your name, address, telephone number and a plea for the binder's return if lost.

Make a page for each of the sections listed in this chapter and fill in as much information as you now have. Keep adding as you progress. The collected information does not yet have to be neat; the important thing is that now you have a place to store your material. As you add pages, as the book fills up, you will have more work to carry with you. When you find a few idle moments, open the book, draft and revise it, bit by bit. Tighten your writing, change words, cut out those that fail to add to your message. Revise and improve.

PARTS OF A BOOK. Most books are divided into three main parts: the preliminary pages or "front matter," the text and the "back matter."

The entire industry is between the writer's thoughts and what the reader sees on the page. — Writers Connection

Pull four or five different types of books off your shelf and compare them as you read further about each part of the book. Older hardbound books usually followed convention.

There are two pages to each sheet or leaf of paper. The "verso" pages are on the left-hand side and are even-numbered, while the "recto" pages are the opposite.

THE FRONT MATTER is that material placed at the beginning of the book. It includes everything up to the start of Chapter One.

ENDPAPERS may be plain or printed, are usually of heavier paper, and are glued to the inside front and back covers of a hardbound (casebound) book. They hold the book together. Occasionally endpapers are printed with relevant maps. Your binder will not require endpapers.

TESTIMONIALS and other sales copy are being seen more and more on the first page of softcover books. This is important sales material. Think about the endorsements and testimonials you might like to have. Leave a blank page here so you can add testimonials and review excerpts to the second edition.

THE HALF TITLE or "bastard title" is often the first printed page found in hardbound books. It contains only the title and it is a right-hand page.

There was a time when books were produced and sold without covers; it was up to the buyers to have the books bound if they wished. The half-title page served to protect the title page and to identify the volume. The custom of including a half-title page persists even though the original reason for it no longer exists.

THE FRONTISPIECE is a photograph found on the reverse of the bastard title page. Often this page is left blank instead or it is used more economically to list other books by the same author.

A book is like a garden carried in a pocket. — Chinese proverb

THE TITLE PAGE is on the right-hand side and lists the full title and subtitle. This page may also include the name of the author or editor, the publisher, whether this is an original or revised edition, and the year.

PEN NAMES seem to be a major preoccupation with new writers. There are few good reasons for changing your name when you write. If you are writing porno books, do not want your boss to know you are moonlighting or wish to conceal your sex (readers seem to prefer female names on romance novels), you might have a reason. But pen names spread you too thin and confuse your readers. As you write, you will establish a following. Using more than one name means establishing a readership for each. If your work is not good enough to sport your name, is the material good enough to print? It may be better to spare the tree.

If you do select a nom de plume, make sure it is not being used by another writer. Check the directories in the reference section of your public library.

Some authors use only their first and middle names as pen names, while others select a maiden name or other family name

Authors using a pseudonym must decide how they want their copyright handled. Should the book be registered in the pen name or the publisher's name? Listing the book in your name will give you away.

You are investing a lot of valuable time in this book. Are you sure you do not want credit for it? Are you sure you want to go through life with an "unlisted name"?

THE COPYRIGHT PAGE or "title page verso" is on the reverse of the title page and is the most important. Here you print the copyright notice (©, year and name of copyright holder), indicate the printing history (number of printings and revisions), the ISBN, the Library of Congress Cataloging-in-Publication Data (including the Library of Congress Catalog number), name and address of the publisher and "printed in the United States of America" (to avoid export complications). Those who know the trade will turn to the copyright page first when picking up a book. Next to the cover, this page is the most important in selling a book, so make it complete.

COPYRIGHT is the subject that most interests potential authors. They want to know how to protect their precious material from others and how much of others' work they can use.

A copyright covers exact printed words, not ideas or thoughts, so you are safe if you just do not copy word-for-word. The copyright law was completely rewritten in 1978, and it will be many years before each and every aspect of it has been interpreted by the courts. The courts seem to deal with each case individually when determining infringement. One test has been whether or not the original work is any less saleable once it has competition from an alleged infringement. Make it a rule never to copy any three words in a row. If your book is not recognizable as being a copy, you should be safe.

A copyright in your name is good for your lifetime plus 50 years (for co-authors, 50 years after the death of the last survivor). If you write a book for an employer (a "work for hire"), the copyright runs 75 years.

YOUR COPYRIGHTED MATERIAL is valuable property, or it may be one day. File copyright forms on all those magazine articles you do not get paid for. You may need an article for inclusion in a book someday, and the expenditure on registration fees will confirm your profession to the Internal Revenue Service.

If you are asked for permission to reprint some of your work, you might allow a reprint of just a section or two, with the stipulation that an editor's note indicates it was used with your permission and came from your book. This will make you look more like an expert and is good publicity for the original work.

A copyright on your book is not only for protection, it is prestigious; it shows you are a professional.

General copyright information and forms can be printed out or downloaded from the Library of Congress website at http://lcweb.loc.gov/copyright. For more information on copyrights, see copyright references listed in the Appendix.

THE DEDICATION PAGE usually contains a short statement, but some authors like to praise their friend(s) in great detail. It is not likely that anyone other than the person(s) mentioned will care about the dedication.

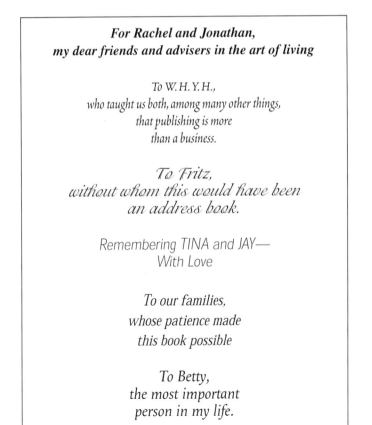

For Rachel and Jonathan,
my dear friends and advisers in the art of living

To W.H.Y.H.,
who taught us both, among many other things,
that publishing is more
than a business.

To Fritz,
without whom this would have been
an address book.

Remembering TINA and JAY—
With Love

To our families,
whose patience made
this book possible

To Betty,
the most important
person in my life.

A search of the books on your shelf will reveal that most books are dedicated to a spouse and the children—the people who put up with the author during the agony (for them both) of writing. This right-hand page was used historically by writers to acknowledge their patrons: the persons or institutions that supported them during the writing.

THE EPIGRAPH PAGE contains a pertinent quotation that sets the tone of the book. Using a separate page for an epigraph in most books is a waste of space.

THE TABLE OF CONTENTS should start on the right-hand side. This page will include the chapter numbers, chapter titles and beginning page numbers. Remember, when buying technical, professional or how-to books, most people turn immediately to the table of contents to check the coverage. Consider this when you name your chapters.

A LIST OF ILLUSTRATIONS is in order if the book is heavily illustrated or if it is a picture-type book. Usually this page is a waste of space. The same goes for a list of tables, especially if they are tied directly to the text.

THE FOREWORD is positioned on the right-hand side and is a pitch for the book by someone other than the author. The name of the contributor appears at the end. Think about who you might get to write this endorsement. Try to find someone well-known in your field. If you include a foreword, note the correct spelling; it is not "forward."

THE PREFACE is written by the author and tells why and how he or she wrote the book. It appears on the right-hand side. If you have an important message and want to be sure the reader receives it, put it in Chapter One, not in the preface or introduction.

ACKNOWLEDGMENTS are a great sales tool. List everyone who helped you in preparation of your manuscript. People love to see their name in print, and each one will become a disciple, spreading the word on your great contribution to literature. They may even purchase a copy. Record names of contributors as you encounter them so that you do not forget anyone. If you list contributors in alphabetical order, they will be less concerned about where they appear on the list.

THE INTRODUCTION tells for whom the book is intended and how the reader should use it.

THE LIST OF ABBREVIATIONS is only required in some very technical books.

THE REPEATED BASTARD TITLE is next, is optional and is a waste of space.

DISCLAIMERS are showing up in more and more books today. See the one in this book as an example.

Obviously, if all the front matter pages listed above were included in your book, you would have a number of pages already. You do not need all these pages, and it is recommended that for most books you do away with all except the title page, copyright page, acknowledgments, table of contents and disclaimer.

THE TEXT of the book is the meaty part on which the front matter and back matter hang. This is the second or main section. Most of the rest of this book concerns the text of your book.

DIVISIONS are sometimes made in long books with distinct but related sections. Their title pages contain the name and number of the section and their reverse sides are usually blank.

Colors fade, temples crumble. empires fall, but wise words endure. — Edward Thorndike

CHAPTERS are used to divide the book into sections, each covering a different aspect of the subject.

CHAPTER TITLES should reveal the subject of the chapter to aid the reader in finding what he or she wants. The reader may be skimming the book in a store pending possible purchase or may be referring back to something he or she read. In either case, you want the chapter description to be as clear as possible.

THE CHAPTER SUBHEAD or paragraph head is a secondary heading or title, usually set in less prominent type than the main heading, to divide the entries under a subject. Subheads can contribute a logical progression, aid in finding needed material and help to break up long chapters.

FOOTNOTES are not needed except in technical publications. If your book will be used as a research tool, the readers may want the footnotes to follow up on the material. Where footnotes must be used, some people recommend they be placed at the end of the chapter or in the appendix, as it is more time-consuming and therefore costly to place them at the bottom of each page.

THE BACK MATTER is all that reference material such as the glossary and index placed at the back of the book. It is less expensive to revise lists at the end of the book when reprinting; try not to print lists subject to change in the text.

THE APPENDIX contains important charts, graphs, lists, etc., and it may be composed of several sections. It is permissible to set this reference material in smaller type. The appendix begins on a right-hand page.

THE ADDENDUM has brief, late additional data. It is printed as part of the book or on a loose sheet.

ERRATA are errors discovered after printing. The list is printed on a separate sheet and may be pasted in or loose.

AUTHOR'S NOTES come next and include additional information in chapter order.

THE GLOSSARY is an alphabetically arranged dictionary of terms peculiar to the subject of the book. Some authors like to save space by combining the glossary and the index. Others define terms in the text as they are encountered. The glossary begins on a right-hand page.

THE BIBLIOGRAPHY lists the reference material or sources you used in writing your book. Some authors place the bibliography at the end of each chapter. When placed at the end of the book, the references may be in appearance order or arranged by subtopic.

THE AFTERWORD is sometimes seen in manuals. Often it is a personal message from the author to the reader wishing the best of luck and/or requesting suggestions for revisions.

COLOPHON is Greek for "finishing touch" and details the production facts by listing the type style, designer, typesetter, printer, kind of paper, plate maker, binder, etc. It is not as common as it once was but is used more and more today in special "labor of love" type publications.

THE INDEX aids the reader in locating specific information in the pages and is particularly important in reference works. Many librarians will not purchase books without indexes. Assembling the index is time-consuming unless you have a word processing program, and the index must be revised every time the book is updated because the page numbers change. The index begins on a right-hand page. It should be positioned near the very end of the book to make it easy to locate.

ORDER BLANK. The last page of the book should contain an offer for more books; place it on a left-hand page—facing out. Some readers will want to purchase a copy for a friend, while others may want a copy for themselves after seeing your book

---

There is more treasure in books than in all the pirates' loot on Treasure Island . . . and the best of all, you can enjoy these riches every day of your life. — Walt Disney at a friend's home or in the library. Make ordering easy for them. This order blank system works.

At Para Publishing, more orders are received on book order blanks than from the general brochure or any other single promotion.

Now that the shell of your book is organized, it is time to work on the inside.

A good book has no ending. — R. D. Cummings

7

GETTING READY TO WRITE
Organization and Research

ORGANIZATION. Many people want to "write a book." Most people have the ability, some have the drive but few have the organization. Therefore, the greatest need is for a simple system, a "road map." In Chapter Six we laid out the structure for your book. In this chapter we will help you get organized.

You may be anxious to put your first words on paper, but important preliminary work remains to be done. The steps described in this chapter can make the difference between a rewarding authoring experience and a frustrating one, a well-thought-out book and a poorly produced manuscript. The basic organizational plan in this book will provide direction, promote drive and uncover ability you never knew existed.

AFFIRMATIONS. Most of the successful people in the world are people with positive attitudes. They are the people who give themselves the "I can" message. Affirmations are positive statements made to yourself that affirm your beliefs. Constant repetition will lead to their acceptance by the mind and establish them in your conscious and subconscious.

The best time for planning a book is while you're doing the dishes. — Agatha Christie

Sports psychologists use this technique for athletes. Think of the pole vaulter going for a new height. The athlete will stand at the beginning of the runway and repeat to himself, "I can go over the top." You need to go through the same process as you begin your project. Begin by making affirmations to yourself as you get up each morning and as you sit down to begin your project. Some statements you might use are:

"I am writing this book."

"My idea for this book is a good one."

"I am in control of my book project."

"I am following through with my book project."

"I am the successful author of a book."

"I am researching this project extensively."

"I am an author."

"My book is being published."

If you repeat these or appropriate affirmations daily, your subconscious will begin to accept them as truths and you will find it easier to take the appropriate action to achieve your goal.

SETTING GOALS that are measurable and have a timetable attached is another process used by successful people. When writing, it is easy to procrastinate. Goals and a timetable will help you stay on schedule and moving in the proper direction. Listing goals and objectives helps you break the project into smaller pieces, making it appear more manageable and realistic.

Just as you need a timetable, you need to be able to measure each step toward your goal. If your goal is very specific, objectives will often suggest themselves. If you want to lose 15 pounds in ten weeks, you will need to lose a pound and a half each week. If you want to write a first draft of 15 chapters in ten weeks, you will have to write an average of a chapter and a half each week.

If your goal is to complete the manuscript of a ten-chapter career counseling book for high school students in one year, some of your objectives might be:

• To spend three months on the preparation and research stage of the book

• For the first draft, to write one chapter per week

• To locate six peer reviewers—two high school counselors, one business personnel director, one concerned parent and two high school students

YOUR WRITING TIMETABLE. You might like to adapt the following timetable to your own needs. After each objective write in a proposed completion date. This will help you see how you are doing. Adjust your plans and expectations if you are not able to keep up with this schedule.

Share this timetable with those close to you. You might even post it next to your mirror or on your home office door. But remember it is only a guide. Getting hung up on your deadlines might lead you to do an inferior or incomplete job. Stress stifles your creativity.

Your first responsibility as an author is to deliver clear, concise and accurate information. Do not skimp in any of these areas just to meet a deadline. The timetable is to help you see how far you have come and how far you have to go.

Reward yourself when you finish each step. Great writers like Mark Twain, Dostoyevsky, Mencken and Dickens worked better under the pressure of deadlines. You probably will, too. A complete timetable provides many incremental deadlines and many incremental completions.

They are able who think they are able. — Virgil

TIMETABLE FOR MANUSCRIPT GENERATION

Projected completion date

INITIATION: GETTING STARTED

Evaluate my motivation
for writing my book

Review my strengths and limitations
and develop a plan

INSPIRATION: BOOK IDEA

Research the competition
and marketability of my topic

Visualize the book and write the
back-cover copy

Negotiate writing time and space
with myself and my family

Make the decision to go ahead
with my project

Write my timetable

PREPARATION: RESEARCH

Set up binder

Set up work area

Gather all books and magazines
related to my topic

Write for further information

Complete the outline of my book

Organize my material with
the "pilot system"

Locate any collaborators needed

Projected completion date

*If you wish to approach
a traditional publisher,
now is the time to send
a query letter.

PERSPIRATION: WRITING

Complete first rough draft

Make list of needed photos
and drawings

Content edit

Conduct more research
to fill in the gaps

Conduct interviews with sources

Complete second draft(s)

VERIFICATION: FINAL EDITING
FOR ACCURACY

Send chapters to experts (peers) in field
for technical review

Complete third draft

Send manuscript to copy editor for
punctuation and grammar review

Complete fourth draft

PUBLICATION: PRODUCTION
AND PROMOTION

*At this point your objectives will depend on the publishing
route you choose. See Chapters Sixteen and Seventeen.

PRODUCTION RATE. Good organization prevents writer's block. A good system prevents procrastination. Set realistic deadlines of so many sections or pages or words per day. It may be helpful to have a friend or family member who will hold you accountable. A regular routine creates momentum—which encourages writing. Without continuity in your writing schedule, you must rebuild momentum each time you sit down to create. When you reach major milestones, give yourself a small reward. You will get a tremendous feeling of pride and accomplishment when you are just a little ahead of schedule.

VISUALIZATION. Another powerful psychological tool is visualization. Sit down and think about what your book will look like. Consider its cover, weight and thickness, the colors, the sales copy on the back cover, etc. See your book in your mind. Imagine holding your book and looking at it. When you visit a bookstore (if that is where you think your book might sell), go to the section where the book would be displayed and visualize your product there with your name on the spine.

Sometimes it helps to have the cover art completed at the beginning of the project. Even a rough sketch of your cover idea hanging up over your computer can be motivating, and it helps you press on with the project.

> *The cover art for Challenges was completed before 20 percent of the text was written. The artist, Robert Howard, interviewed Mindy for nearly two hours about the theme and the feeling of the text. The art captured the spirit of the book so well that it gave Mindy and her co-authors the inspiration to push on to complete the manuscript.*

Your mental picture of your book may change as you progress with the manuscript. But by forming a mental image of your future book, you have already begun to realize your goal.

ORGANIZE YOUR WORKSPACE. The successful home office workspace is the result of careful attention to space, furnishings, storage and equipment. You should locate the workspace where you will be undisturbed, comfortable and close to your writing tools.

Set up a writing sanctuary in a spare room, wall unit, closet or a corner of the living room. Keep all your writing materials and research tools there. Your creative writing time is precious; do not waste it in setting up your work area each day.

Most people today have a computer available to them. If you don't, you should consider purchasing one. You will find that technology will greatly enhance your productivity and enjoyment of the process. Writing and editing is more efficient with a computer and with an Internet connection; the libraries of the world are literally at your fingertips.

FINDING TIME. Time or lack of it is the most frequently heard excuse for not writing. But somehow we always find the time for those things most important to us. We just put them first. Often you can fit in an hour of writing time each day by completing other chores faster. Or you might get up one hour earlier each day. This has definite advantages, since the house is quiet, the telephone does not ring and the early morning is one of the most creative and productive times for most writers. Once you gather momentum in your project, you will find it easy to get up early; you won't even miss that hour of sleep. View writing as a serious job. Use discipline. You must put this hour first and not let anything or anyone interfere with it. The affirmation "Right now my book is my priority. I will work on it (#) hours per day," may help you stay on track.

How much time do you spend watching television, eating out, talking on the telephone, browsing in stores or socializing with people you do not really enjoy? Why not use some of this time for your project? There are 8,760 hours in a year. Surely you can allocate some of them to your writing project.

Bargain with your family for uninterrupted time. Just one interruption can blow your concentration for 20 minutes— and ruin your writing day. It is difficult to pick up where you left off.

BEST TIME OF DAY TO WRITE. Write when you are the most creative. For some authors, this means getting up early. Others write better in the evening. It does not matter when you write as long as you write regularly during your most creative period without interruption.

Set up a schedule and try to write at least one hour each day. Writing less or taking off for too many days between creative periods will force you to waste time refreshing your memory; you will forget where you left off.

RESEARCHING YOUR SUBJECT will fill in the gaps in personal experience. Research is simply reading, interviewing, making notes and rearranging the gathered pertinent information. The craft of nonfiction writing is based upon research. Most kinds of fiction require research as well. The best research usually comes from original sources such as diaries, historical societies, letters, journals, old newspaper files and on-the-spot observation. Here are several ways to find the information you need.

Researchers. If you do not have the time to do all the required research, it is possible to hire someone to do it for you. But good research is detective work. One fact may lead to another idea, so it is best to do most research yourself. However, researchers can be helpful when you have to find specific information that might require time you don't have.

Library. The importance of using the library cannot be overemphasized. All research must begin there and most of the required information will be found within its walls. But there are different types of libraries and each has specific

---

If my doctor told me I had only six months to live, I wouldn't brood. I'd type a little faster. — Isaac Asimov kinds of references. You won't find much fiction in a college library. Law libraries have every law book you are likely to need and not much else. The public library may cover more subjects, but only lightly because it must serve the general public. Generally, you will find three important sources of information there:

1. The card catalog listing all its books by title, author and subject. Most libraries have abandoned the cards in favor of computers. The listings are viewed on terminals.

2. Indexes such as the *Reader's Guide*, catalogs of articles, essays, reports and other information.

3. General references such as encyclopedias, dictionaries and directories.

4. Libraries with Internet access sometimes have subscriptions to costly databases you do not have at home.

Be a detective. When you run out of leads, ask the reference librarian. Libraries carry hundreds of indexes, listings and source books. Gather everything ever written on your subject. Load yourself up with so much material you will have to decide what to leave out. Overdo it and you can be proud to know that you have covered the subject completely.

Borrow from the library or purchase all the recent magazines in your subject area. Tear out or photocopy all the important articles and underline their most important parts. Always write the name of the periodical and the issue date at the top of the page, so you will know the origin of the article and how old the information is.

Find all the recent books on your topic and buy them or get them from the library. Check *Books in Print* or an on-line bookstore such as Amazon.com for books currently available. Comb used book stores for older books. Most books should be purchased and added to your personal library. (While shopping in the used bookstore, pick up references such as a

---

Writing is the art of applying the seat of the pants to the seat of the chair. — Mary Heaton Vorse thesaurus and a style manual. A few years old, they are much cheaper and still perfectly good.)

Some books and magazines in the library will be restricted to the Reference Room. When you cannot check them out, make notes of small bits of information and use the photocopy machine to record longer pieces. Be sure to have rolls of coins, because many libraries have a limit on the amount of change they will give. If you wish to use photos and drawings of material with expired copyrights, use photocopier for the drawings and reshoot the photos with a camera (more on this later). Even if the copyright has not expired, make a photocopy of valuable illustrations to guide you in your research. Photocopy useful parts of checked-out books and magazines at the local copy center. They usually charge less than the library.

Make good use of your library time by bringing along a list of questions to be answered. Do not get sidetracked by recreational reading.

Write for information. After exhausting the library's information, move on to the many other available sources.

Read through the magazines in your field and write to every pertinent advertiser for more information on their products. Many will supply you with valuable information on the product area. Use the quick order "bingo" cards in the magazines and write short requests to the rest. Later you may write to people and companies for more specific information. Right now you are just fishing.

Request *Selected U.S. Government Publications* from the Superintendent of Documents, USGPO, PO Box 1821, Washington, DC 20402. This is a monthly catalog of government publications. Many of these pamphlets are also available at U.S. Government bookstores in the larger cities. Check the White Pages or log on to http://www. access.gpo.gov where you can access government information products.

University Microfilms (300 North Zeeb Road, Ann Arbor, MI 48106) has over 150,000 doctoral dissertations in every

ᔓ⁄ᔓᔓ Para Publishing

P.O. Box 8206, Santa Barbara, CA 93118-8206 USA

September 17, 1999

High Tech Book, Inc.
Promotion Department
454 Silicon Street
Cupertino, CA 95014

<u>Examination copy request</u>

Ladies and Gentlemen:

Your book, *Ghostwriting for Fun and Profit* by Christine Nolt, has been recommended to us as a resource which should be listed in our new book on methods of writing books, To be considered for inclusion, please send the following.

1. A review copy of the book ("hurt" copies are acceptable),
2. The current list price.
3. Ordering information (bookstore or mail order address),
4. A book description in 200 words or less (a brochure is acceptable), and
5. Photocopies of at least two independent reviews.

Para Publishing has a growing line of writing and publishing resource books. We expect the audience for this new book to be quite large. Any book mentioned in the text should experience a number of sales.

We are working under a very tight schedule. Please give this request your immediate attention.

Sincerely,

PARA PUBLISHING

Dan Poynter

Dan Poynter
Publisher

DFP/ms
Enclosure: Para Publishing brochure

Tel: (805) 968-7277; Fax: (805) 968-1379; Cellular: (805) 448-9009; Fax-On-Demand: (805) 968-8947
e-mail: DanPoynter@ParaPublishing.com   Web site: http://www.ParaPublishing.com

The letter used for this book

field. They can run a computer search on any key word and provide a list of papers in which that word appears. Then you may order copies of the dissertations you want. Tapping distant databases with a computer is covered in Chapter Eight.

The Internet and the World Wide Web offer publishers unlimited opportunities to do research for books, conduct business transactions, promote books and sell books. If you like the library, you will love the Internet; it provides access to an incredible amount of information and makes it easy to find. You can do your banking and trace UPS and FedEx packages. Forget postage; you can blast information on your book to selected interested parties with the price of a local telephone call. And, it is inexpensive to set up a website listing all your books and services. Customers can order your books with a credit card via e-mail. This is making money while you sleep.

If you are not already on the web, check out a workshop or adult education class in your community. Learning how to use the Internet is easier than learning how to program your VCR. Or hire a private tutor such as a college student who is proficient and who uses the Internet to research his or her school projects.

Check out the Para Publishing website at http://www.para publishing.com/books/para/890. It will lead you to more book publishing sites. There are over 450 pages of resources.

Many documents are not copyrighted. Normally you will be gathering material, blending it, boiling it down and extracting information of interest to your specific group of readers. However, there will be times when you find a piece of material you simply must have. If you want to determine whether some material is protected under either the current or pre-1978 law, the Copyright Office will conduct a search for you. Send them as much information as possible, such as the author, title, publisher and publication date. The cost is approximately $10 per hour, and they should be able to make two searches per hour. Government and military publications are in the public domain. Even if they were not, they would probably be covered by the Freedom of Information Act. If you really need a piece of material, military or civilian, ask for permission. It is safer and cheaper than hiring a lawyer later to prove you have a right to it.

A good way to make your request for permission to use someone's copyrighted material is to photocopy the material you want to use, circle just that part, and send it to the copyright holder, along with a letter explaining how you want to use the material and asking for a release. Be sure to ask for the world rights to reprint the material in case your book is picked up by a foreign publisher. Wait until you receive a reply in writing before you proceed with publishing. Sometimes you will not be granted permission or the price will be very high. Also the copyright holder may require you to note the source and that permission was given.

The Yellow Pages and the telephone often uncover a great wealth of information. You can always find someone with information or a lead to information.

Attend instruction courses at a local college. Keep up with the latest technology. Find out what is on the minds of the other students—and answer their questions with your book.

Press pass. Now that you are researching, you are a member of the print media and will be able to attend a lot of related events free. When visiting trade shows, use your new business card to get a press pass, media packet and preferential treatment.

Interviews with the experts will uncover inside details and current information. In most nonfiction book writing, interviews are used to fill in the gaps. As you draft your book, questions should be written in the margin and then transferred to a separate sheet.

You may write to or call the expert. Make an appointment so your interviewee will be relaxed and will have the calendar cleared for you. Identify yourself and your project so the person understands who you are and what you want. Be prepared. The interview will go smoother and faster if you have a list of specific questions. Formulate your questions so they cannot be answered with a straight "yes" or "no." Make your expert explain or qualify his or her answers. Check the questions off as you proceed through the interview. Some answers will lead to further questions.

Do not talk about yourself during the interview unless you are asked. You won't learn if you are talking. One of your major missions in an interview is to make a friend or acquaintance of your contact. He or she is a resource and you may wish to call back later for more leads or verification of facts.

OUTLINE your book so you can see where you are going. This is one of the most important steps in the production of your material, so take your time and give it a lot of thought. A carefully thought-through outline will save you a lot of work later when you start writing your first draft. It will help clarify what kind of research you need to do. It is another tool to help keep your project on track.Make up a list of chapters and note what you plan to cover in each.

This project may take from a couple of days to a couple of months. Once you have completed the first draft of your outline, set it aside for a while so you can mull it over. You want it to be complete, ordered and as close to the final outline of the book as possible. The more complete and ordered your outline, the easier it will be to write the first draft.

After all, most writing is done away from the typewriter, away from the desk. I'd say it occurs in the quiet, silent moments, while you're walking or shaving or playing a game, or whatever, or even talking to someone you're not vitally interested in. You're working, your mind is working, on this problem in the back of your head. — Henry Miller

ORGANIZE YOUR MATERIAL WITH THE "PILOT SYSTEM."

Sort all your research material and "pile it" as required. Decide on your chapter titles and, using scissors, tape and staples, sort all this copied material into the applicable chapter piles. During your library research, you must have written down a number of interesting observations, many of your own experiences. Add your own notes to the piles. Laying out the piles is fun. You are only getting ready to work, and this layout makes the big job look like many small jobs. Now take the papers from your "horizontal filing cabinet" and spread out the individual chapters. The piles will probably completely fill the living room. Pick an interesting pile, any one, not necessarily the first, and go through it, underlining important points and writing in your additional comments. Write out longer thoughts on a tablet and file them in order in the pile.

This floor spread will enable you to see the whole-interrelated project, lending excitement and encouragement—a great incentive. Move the piles around to insure a good, logical flow of thought and to avoid duplication of copy. Discard unnecessary and duplicate material.

This use of information from other sources is not plagiarism; it is research. Your notes insure that you will not leave out any important points. However, you will be entertained as you compare what various authors say about the same item. The similarities are often remarkable. You will come across the same words and phrases time and again.

IMPROVE THE MATERIAL by continually reviewing it and boiling it down. As you read what others say on a particular point, your memory will be jogged. You will have additional points, a clearer explanation or an illustrative story.

Keep your mind tuned in to your subject. Stay alert to information that may be useful. Write it down and date

---

Writers often say, truthfully, that they are as much at work away from their desks as in the act of writing itself.
— Paul Horgan

the scrap of paper. Be thorough! Consider what will be on the reader's mind and answer those questions in convincing detail. Use imagination in writing, not in research. Be accurate. Just because you find some information in print, do not assume it is correct. Double-check all facts—do not perpetuate a myth. You are about to commit history—it is a great responsibility. If you disagree with another author, you can always say, "Some people believe . . ." and then tell it your way. You have the advantage of the most recent information, since you came last.

Carry paper and pen with you at all times, especially when working, running or engaging in any solo activity. This is the time to think, create, compose; this is when there is no one around to break your train of thought. Some authors keep a pad or tape recorder in their car and compose while commuting. When you are confined, captive, isolated, you have nothing else to do but create. Make use of any available time. A lot of good material develops while attending dull meetings.

Some people like to work with a small pocket tape recorder, but remember that someone must transcribe this noise onto paper. If you often dictate letters and have a secretary to transcribe your tapes, this may be the most comfortable and most efficient method for you.

When a particularly original thought or creative approach hits you, write it down or record it immediately, or you will lose it. Keep on thinking and keep on note-taking. Add your thoughts and major pieces to the piles. Draw up a list of questions as they come to mind, so that you will remember to conduct the research to answer them.

TEST YOUR MATERIAL with lectures, demonstrations, seminars and/or magazine articles. Gain experience and get feedback from your audience. Adopt what works and modify what does not.

Some of the material for *Choices* grew out of a class taught in several Santa Barbara high schools. The exercises were developed and tested with the teenagers. If an exercise worked, it was added to the manuscript. If it didn't, it was thrown out.

By now, you should be organized. You have begun your research and your project is taking on its direction. The next chapter offers some suggestions that will make the coming work easier and more rewarding.

History does not repeat itself. Nonfiction writers repeat each other.

8

TOOLS OF THE TRADE

All you really need to create a book are paper and pencil. A desk with good lighting, a computer, photocopy machine, cordless telephone, scanner, Internet access, camera, reference books and a filing cabinet will make the job easier. When you shop for equipment, buy the best you can afford. You will have it for some time, and nothing is worse than a cheap tool which performs poorly or which breaks just when you need it. Plumbers have the best tools, and so should wordsmiths.

Office machinery has created a revolution in the process of gathering and writing information. The machines cut out the laborious, repetitive work and allow you to concentrate on the creative aspects of the writing project.

REFERENCE BOOKS. Dictionaries and other reference books are much less expensive at used-book stores. The books you should have are listed in Chapter Ten.

OFFICE FURNITURE, too, can be purchased much more cheaply secondhand. Make sure your desk and chair are good quality, comfortable and fit you.

We have discussed manual methods of writing a book. Now, since so many people have access to computers and other office machinery, we will describe their use in manuscript generation. Consider how the following items might be useful to you.

COPY MACHINE. The photocopy machine is a very useful tool for research. When setting off for the library in the search for information, always take a pocketful of coins for the copy machine. Photocopy the lists and other useful information you find rather than hand-copying them onto index cards. Use the same method when doing research at home. Build the information piles with these photocopied notes as described in Chapters Seven and Nine. Use the "pilot system."

Of course, the copy machine is also useful for making duplicates of your manuscript. An extra copy of your work should always be stashed in a safe place. And you will need copies of sections of the manuscript to send off for peer review.

Use the local copy shop or purchase your own machine. To find a copy shop, get out the *Yellow Pages* and look under "Copying & Duplicating." Call all the shops in your area to compare prices. Usually those shops situated near colleges are the most competitive.

Prices of copy machines have fallen tremendously in the last few years. If you are making copies on a daily basis, owning your own machine will pay for itself very quickly. Copies will be cheaper, you will save gas and, more important, you will save time. You will be able to work when you want to, and this means you will finish book sections and other projects sooner. It is also more private.

COMPUTERS. The computer is your most important tool. You will use it for Internet research, writing, typesetting and promotion. Get the best you can afford.

COMPUTER RESEARCH. Nearly all the resources, information and people you need to contact can be found on the Web. Today, many writers and researchers avoid the trip to the library and do all their research from home. Copying is easier. Much (non-copyrighted) material can be copy-and-pasted into the manuscript.

When Dan Poynter was revising The Expert Witness Handbook, *he needed the latest edition of the* Federal Rules of Evidence. *He found the document on the Cornell University website. A quick copy and paste saved him a trip to the law library, photocopying and a lot of retyping.*

With a modem and a telephone line, a computer may be used to search distant databases for information. For example, you might want a printout of all the patents issued in a certain area. A search of the *PATSEARCH Database* might cost $20 to $70. That may sound like a lot, but compare it with what it would cost to visit a distant patent library and spend days making a physical search. Databases exist on every conceivable subject. Small firms specializing in database searches are springing up everywhere. Check the Yellow Pages.

Also see the discussion on page 92 with regard to the use of the Internet and World Wide Web to obtain information.

E-mail is the fastest way to send research questions and is invaluable when working with a collaborator.

COMPUTER WRITING. Computers improve writing immeasurably. There is a big difference between a manuscript written, edited and typed by hand and one that has been worked over as many times as necessary to pull every last bit of creativity out of the prose and to wring out every redundant phrase or unnecessary word.

People who input original material into a computer usually find that their style improves. They can edit while

---

Good writing does not come from fancy word processors or expensive typewriters or special pencils or hand-crafted quill pens. Good writing comes from good thinking.
— Ann Loring in *Write and Sell Your TV Drama*

they type, catch extra words, break up long sentences and reword for clarity.

Word processing reduces procrastination. You can start a big project anywhere simply by entering random thoughts. Once you have something down on paper, you can go back and add, edit or clean up your prose.

Books are much easier to write on a computer. During the editing phase, sentences, whole paragraphs and even entire chapters will be moved as the text is organized and refined.

MS Word will mark the revised portions of a document in the margin to indicate which sections need a second look. Then on the final printout, the revision marks are deleted. This feature is especially useful when there is more than one person working on the manuscript.

Speech recognition software. Programs like IBM's *Via Voice* and Dragon System's *NaturallySpeaking* require a lot of computer power (Pentium II-300) but they can speed "writing" and save you from carpal tunnel syndrome! Check out the websites: www.naturalspeech.com and www.ibm.com.

COMPUTER EDITING is done on the screen before the manuscript is committed to paper. The spelling and grammar programs in *MS-Word* are quite good. The final draft of the manuscript still needs to be proofed but after using these programs, there is much less rewriting to do.

THE THRILL OF VICTORY—THE AGONY OF DELETE. Save and back up your work often. There is nothing more frustrating than writing a whole chapter and then finding that your computer has "eaten it." This can occur when your computer "freezes" and you have shut down or "force quit," then find that you've lost changes to your text because you haven't saved it or backed it up.

When Mindy was working on the book Challenges, *there was one particular chapter that had her stymied. She could not figure out which approach to take. After*

*spending three days researching and reading— ZAP,
THE INSPIRATION HIT. She raced to the computer and
spent three hours banging out the chapter. She finished
with a great feeling of accomplishment for she knew it
was just right! She sighed in relief, pushed the button
for review and was faced with a blank screen. In her
intense concentration, she had forgotten to store
the document.*

BOOK INDEXING is a snap with a computer. Gone are the
index cards, alphabetizing and retyping. Just build your index
as you read the final proof of the typeset book, and autosort
to make sure the entries are in correct alphabetical order.

COMPUTER TYPESETTING. There are two ways to set type
with your computer.

Use a laser printer to set 600 dpi (dots per inch) or higher
laser type. Many books are typeset this way today and the
printers know how to adjust their cameras and presses to
clean up the rough edges on the type.

*Dan Poynter was the first publisher to laser-typeset a
book. Word Processors & Information Processing was
set on a Xerox 9700 Electronic Printer in 1982. Since
then he has typeset all his books using the computer.
He estimates this has saved him thousands of hours
and untold sums of money. This one technological
advancement has made writing and self-publishing
available to almost everyone.*

Doing your typesetting in-house will save a great deal in
both time and money. In fact, you can save enough money on
typesetting one or two books to buy all the equipment—and
you have the computer to write and edit the manuscript.
Typesetting a 150-page book may take from two to four days.

Or, you may draft and edit your manuscript on your
computer and then give it to your printer on disk. The result
is crisper, higher-resolution type.

NOTEBOOK COMPUTERS. Portable (notebook) computers allow you to work away from your office. Check the keyboards and screens closely, and make sure they are comfortable and easy to use.

THE NEXT MOVE. If you do not already have a computer, it is time to buy. Start with word processing and look into other programs later. The most popular word-processing program is *MS-Word*.

Your computer choice is between the PC and Macintosh systems. Each has advantages and disadvantages over the other and neither is a bad choice. Bear in mind, however, that Macintosh has less than 5 percent of the installed user base and therefore there are fewer software programs and peripherals available for it.

FACSIMILE MACHINES. The fax machine speeds manuscript compilation and proofing but many of the tasks are being replaced by e-mail.

TAPE RECORDERS are useful for recording notes as well as for interviewing. These recorders may be hand-held, designed for dictation or even voice-activated. Some people carry these "note-takers" when they are doing their "thinking" about their books, to record thoughts and inspirations while they are fresh and exciting. If your most creative times seem to be during your drive to work each morning, a tape recorder is a much safer way to capture your ideas than jotting them down on a pad in rush-hour traffic.

As illustrated in the Jim Comiskey story in Chapter Twelve, your information may be recorded on a tape recorder if you speak slowly. If you tend to think in spurts or are used to a dictating machine, you may wish to invest in one.

It is a lot easier to use a tape recorder than pad and pencil when conducting interviews. The machine ensures that you have all the information recorded and you can review your tape for different sections of your book. Some people tend to open up more when you use a tape recorder instead of taking notes. If your interviewee is a fast speaker, note-taking can be frustrating for you both. But also be sensitive to the person who is intimidated by a tape recorder. If you sense inhibition, turn off the recorder and go back to note-taking. Always ask the person you are interviewing for permission to record the conversation.

For interviewing over the telephone, pickups are available from stores such as Radio Shack. Some telephone answering machines also have the ability to record two-way conversations. Be sure you have received permission to record the telephone conversation with your interviewee before proceeding.

CAMERAS. If your manuscript requires photographs and you do not already have one, you will want to get a good camera. Get a digital model so you can download the photos directly into your manuscript

MACHINERY. As you do more writing, look for labor-saving machinery to make the most of your efforts. Personal computers, photocopy and fax machines, cordless telephones and postage meters will save you time. They are much better buys than an employee, and you will find that with depreciation, machines are not very expensive.

If I had eight hours to chop down a tree, I'd spend six sharpening my ax. — Abraham Lincoln

Writing is a solitary occupation. Family, friends, and society are the natural enemies of the writer. He must be alone, uninterrupted, and slightly savage if he is to sustain and complete an undertaking. — Lawrence Clark Powell

9

HOW TO WRITE A BOOK

It is not our intention to teach you the mechanics of writing; there are far too many good books available on working with words. Some are listed in the Appendix. However, this chapter outlines a proven writing system and reveals a number of inside tricks, tips and techniques used by successful authors.

If you haven't already done so, you must decide where your talents lie and what parts of your project you want to perform by yourself. Are you an idea person or are you a writer? Do you enjoy writing or do you want to be a published author without the "pain" of writing? If you plan to do most of the writing yourself, try the following system. You may plan to hire help, but unless you are hiring a ghostwriter or contract writer, you will still do most of the organization of the project yourself. Read this chapter in order to understand the system and consider the organization.

[handwritten in margin: I am the idea person— not the writer]

WRITING THE BOOK YOURSELF. Creating your own material is easy if you have a system; all it takes is organization and discipline. Following the system outlined below, creating copy becomes challenging fun and allows you to easily see the progress you are making—which is encouraging. This method may be of some help in writing fiction, but it was developed specifically for nonfiction.

Work is the price you pay for money.

TO GET STARTED, assemble your notes by cutting, sorting and taping. Take one chapter from your "pilot system" piles and lay the paper strips out in logical order. Connect the strips with Magic Transparent Tape. When adding your thoughts, never write on the back of a piece of paper. You want to be able to lay out all your materials where you can see them.

WRITE from the pasted strips. Read the whole pasted-up section to grasp the overall theme. Then boil the material down and use your own words. Think about the section and how you might improve the message. Can't you say it better with fewer words?

Do not just write from the strips sentence by sentence. Some of the material is not yours so that might be plagiarism. For organization, list the main points and rearrange the pieces. If you are having trouble with a section, arrange it as best you can and come back to it later. If you still cannot bring the message together with a few well-chosen sentences, you may have to call another expert for his or her explanation of the subject matter. If you cannot reach the colleague or are otherwise still having trouble with a section, put the pile back on the floor and pick up an easier, more interesting pile. Skip around.

You have selected your subject and your audience—do not lose sight of who you are writing for. Talk to your audience, follow your outline and make sure your manuscript says what you want it to say—completely but concisely.

Many books should start off with an "action" chapter. Like the introductory part of a speech, the beginning of a book should arouse readers and whet their appetite. Too many authors want to start from the "beginning" and put a history chapter first. Readers want to know where to and how to. Do not lose them in the first chapter.

If you want to be a writer, forget it. If you have to be a writer, you just might make it. — Sidney Sheldon

Do not start to write with Chapter One—to do so makes book writing look like an impossible mountain climb (with you at the very bottom). Select the chapter pile that looks the shortest, easiest or most fun. It may be the smallest pile or the most interesting one. Once you have written it, take the next most interesting chapter and so on. Soon you will be past the halfway mark. You will be encouraged and will gather momentum. Using this approach, you will probably find yourself writing the first chapter last. This is as it should be, as the first chapter usually serves as an introduction. You cannot know what it should say until the rest of the work is drafted. Many authors wind up completely rewriting and reslanting the first chapter because they wrote it first.

Do not be concerned with your writing style the first time around. The important thing is to get your thoughts down. Often these first impressions are the best; they are complete, natural and believable. Later you will make corrections, additions and deletions. Major changes will require rewriting, while minor corrections will only need some proofing marks. Sentences and paragraphs will be added by cutting and pasting in the new material. With your book set up in loose-leaf binder form, it will be easy to add material.

As you input the first draft, and later as you review it, you will decide whole paragraphs need to be moved.

If you lack a certain piece of information, a number or a fact, leave a blank space, put a note in the margin or type "***" and go on. The asterisks stick out in a manuscript, and you can always conduct a "search" for them just to make sure you have filled in all the blanks. Keep your momentum going. Similarly, if you find yourself repeating material, make a note in the margin so you can compare it later with the sentences in the other location.

Remember, writing from notes is not plagiarism but solid, thorough research—an efficient system made possible by

---

*Begin every story in the middle. The reader doesn't care how
it begins, he wants to get on with it.* — Louis L'Amour

Xerox. Practically every nonfiction book is simply a repackaging and updating of existing material with the author's personal experience and prejudices incorporated. Draft one complete section (often several paragraphs) at a time if possible. One chapter at a time is better. Most beginning authors must work at regular jobs and are able to devote only a short period each day to their writing. But the more time you can put into each piece of the book, the better, as there will be greater continuity, less duplication and clearer organization. If you can only do a small section at a time, try arranging the pieces in the evening, reviewing them in the early morning, thinking about them while commuting and then inputting the whole section into your computer when you arrive home.

If you can, take two weeks off from work, shut out all distractions and become totally involved in the manuscript. Do not pick up the mail or answer the telephone. Eat when hungry, sleep when tired and forget the clock except as a gauge of your pace. Keep up the pressure and keep on inputting text into your computer. Pace yourself at, say, one chapter per day. You should not have to force yourself to write, but you do need organization and discipline.

Do not throw out your materials once your draft is finished. Put them in a cardboard carton. Someone may ask where you found a particular piece of information, and you will want to be able to locate it

LAY OUT THE BINDER. Now that you are generating copy, you need a place to store it. Add divider cards to your binder corresponding to the chapters you have selected. Insert the rough pages you have input as you complete them. They should be numbered by chapter and page. For example, "6-14" would be page 14 in Chapter Six. As the piles come off the floor, cross the desk and flow through the word processor into

---

There is no such thing as a publishable first draft. — William Targ the binder, you will gain a great feeling of accomplishment. You must decide now whether secondary matter is of value or just window dressing. An index, appendix, bibliography or directory may add to the usefulness of the book or may cost more than it is worth to include. It depends on the subject and your treatment of it. But all these items should be decided upon early, so a running list can be maintained as you do your research. Remember that some books are composed of nothing but lists.

Soon you will have a partial manuscript, something tangible to carry around. This makes you feel proud and allows you to work on your manuscript away from home. If your book is short, you might collect all your material in the binder, bypassing the piles of notes.

It is wise to photocopy your manuscript periodically for storage in another location. If the fruit of your creativity were misplaced or destroyed in a fire, you would suffer both financially and emotionally.

WRITING STYLE. Before writing a magazine article, it is important to read several back issues to pick up that publication's style. The same technique works in writing a book. Begin your writing session by reading a few chapters by a writer you admire.

Writing is a communication art. You should not try to impress. Write as you speak, avoiding big words where small ones will do. Most people use regularly only 800 to 1,000 of the some 26,000 English words available to them. Use simple sentences and be precise in your selection of words. Vary sentence and paragraph length and favor the shorter ones. Try to leave yourself out of the copy: avoid overusing the word "I."

Don't get it right. Get it written, then get it right.
— Goren George Moberg in *Writing in Groups*

Use action nouns and verbs. Help the reader draw a mental picture by introducing sight, sound, smell, touch and taste to your copy. Be precise. Avoid superlatives and overuse of adverbs and adjectives. Study newspaper writing and place the words you wish to emphasize at the beginning of the sentence. The important sentence should start the paragraph, and the main paragraph should head the chapter.

Relax, talk on paper, be yourself. Explain each section in your own words as if you were trying to help a friend who is new to the subject. Do not use contractions in your writing as you do in your speech as they're (there is one now) more difficult to read. "Which" and "that" can often be left out to the benefit of the sentence. Keep your writing short. In magazine writing you may be paid by the word, but in book writing additional words have a way of costing you, so edit out the junk.

Like a speech, every paragraph should have a beginning, a middle and an end. Use smooth transitions from paragraph to paragraph to make your writing flow. The first sentence of the paragraph is called the "topic sentence"—stay with one subject per paragraph.

Use proper terms; do not start a new language. Steer away from highly technical language; you will only turn off your readers.

One technique for educating your readers is to use the proper term and then follow it with the more popular word in parentheses. Educating the reader as you progress through the book is preferable to making him or her stop and refer to a glossary.

Anticipate trends to keep your work up-to-date. Use metric and nonsexist terms wherever possible. Cookbooks in the United States may not be ready to switch to metric and books on printing will deal with 17" x 22" presses and 5½" x 8½" books for a long time, but many measurements can be

---

Less is more. — Robert Browning

avoided by using comparisons. For example, instead of telling a parachutist to prepare for landing at "30 feet," say at "treetop height." The comparison is clearer, anyway.

As a published author, you are considered an expert. Whether you are writing fiction or nonfiction, you must be accurate. You have a responsibility to find out what happened (or in fiction, what could have happened) at that particular time and place.

Be a professional, and give the readers their money's worth. Your material will be used by others in coming years, and you will be quoted. If you are accurate now, you will not be embarrassed later by the written legend you have created.

Writing is hard work; it is an intellectual and emotional workout. Some authors enjoy the discipline writing requires, but more have a greater appreciation for the results.

Move through your notes and reduce those piles of research materials to pages in your binder. The next step is to clean up what you have written: Revise and edit.

STORYBOARDING. For fiction writers, the process is slightly different. Instead of taping strips of paper together, you may want to use a storyboard system.

Set up a system to keep track of what is going on in your novel (or story or play). Use a bulletin board with cards attached or a notebook such as the one described here.

A storyboard gives you a visual prop for your storyline. As your ideas are generated and the plot begins to take shape, your storyboard allows you the freedom to add and move events around, always being cognizant of chronological order. So when the idea for a great scene hits, you can figure out where to add it to the manuscript.

It is essential to keep track of your chronology (what year is it? If the heroine was 15 when your story began, how old is she now?), the facts (If your story takes place in 1885, could

---

What a heavy oar the pen is, and what a strong current ideas are to row in. — Gustave Flaubert there be a telephone in the house?) and the situation (Was George at the fateful meeting, or did you place him in Siberia at the time it took place?).

You will find it helpful to have something to refer to when the action gets heavy and complicated. And when you finish your first draft, like your nonfiction writing colleagues, you will need to edit, edit, edit . . .

Don't write merely to be understood. Write so that you cannot possibly be misunderstood.
— Robert Louis Stevenson

10

REVISE AND EDIT, edit, edit . . .

REVISING AND EDITING your manuscript involves refining, adding, rearranging and cutting material as well as checking punctuation and spelling. Some writers say drafting a book consists of 10 percent writing and 90 percent rewriting.

You will have to complete at least four drafts to make sure that your work is as thorough, concise, correct and readable as you can make it. These drafts are labeled as follows:

- First draft — rough draft
- Second draft(s) — content edit
- Third draft — peer review
- Fourth draft — copy edit

The first or rough draft was described in Chapter Nine. The object was to compile the research materials, put them into your own words and get them onto the hard disk. Now you can see where the holes are. The project is quantified and you can see what needs to be done.

If at first you don't succeed, you are running about average.
— M. H. Anderson

Second draft: content edit. Perform this step yourself. It is not uncommon for this edit to take as much effort as writing the original manuscript. You must be extremely critical at this point, so take your time. Look for places in the manuscript that need more information or more attention. Review all your original research material to make sure nothing has been left out. Do any further research necessary to fill the holes that appear. Delete the parts that are irrelevant to your purpose. Keep the theme and goal of your book in mind and do not stray from them. Clean up what you have written.

Do not try to do all the rewriting at one time. Carry your manuscript with you in a binder and do what you can when you can. Editing can be fun, and it is far easier than the original writing. You have the rough draft on paper, now all you have to do is refine it. Skip around and work on whatever section interests you. Whenever you get a good idea, write it down and put it in the appropriate place in your three-ring binder.

Whenever you lose momentum, re-enter a page with a lot of handwritten notes. This clean-up work has a stimulating effect.

It may take several drafts to polish your work. So what is defined as the second draft could amount to a number of iterations (this book went through eight-second drafts).

I can't understand how anyone can write without rewriting everything over and over again. I scarcely ever re-read my published writings, but if by chance I come across a page, it always strikes me: All this must be rewritten; this is how I should have written it. — Leo Tolstoy

SECOND DRAFT EVALUATION

You have completed the second draft editing stage when you can answer "yes" to all the following questions:

_____ 1. Does my manuscript have all the information needed to give the reader a clear understanding of the subject?

_____ 2. Is the information included the most current?

_____ 3. Is the manuscript easy to read and understand?

_____ 4. Is the order of the material logical and not redundant?

_____ 5. Is my manuscript targeted to the market I defined when beginning my book?

If you are writing a work of fiction, ask yourself these questions as well:

_____ 1. Are the times and locations of my story always clear?

_____ 2. Are my characters memorable and do they have distinct personalities?

_____ 3. Have any of my characters been lost in the manuscript? Will the reader have trouble tracking them?

_____ 4. Is there a strong conflict that continues to build interest?

_____ 5. Is my theme clear without being preachy?

_____ 6. Does the story entertain?

REFERENCE BOOKS. Some of the reference books you will need at this point are:

- A stylebook such as the *Chicago Manual of Style,* 14th Edition, the *U.S. Government Printing Office Style Manual* or the *Associated Press Stylebook.*
- A good dictionary (and if you are dealing with a specialized subject, also get a dictionary on that subject.)
- A book on grammar, punctuation and style, such as *Write Right!* or *The Gregg Reference Manual*
- A thesaurus or dictionary of synonyms and antonyms.
- A book on usage, such as *Fowler's Modern English Usage* or Bernstein's *The Careful Writer: A Modern Guide to English Usage.*

These references will back up the spelling and grammar programs in your word processing program.

Third draft: peer review. Once you have your manuscript as complete and correct in content as you feel it needs to be, it is time to send it out to other experts in your field to review for technical proofing.

Begin by making a list of everyone you know who might provide valuable input for your manuscript. You may want some of these people to review the entire manuscript; others may only have information on one area or chapter.

Once you have received commitments to review the draft, make photocopies and ask the experts to make notes right on their copy. Enclose a self-addressed, stamped envelope and remember to give them credit in the Acknowledgments. With the peer review, you will not only produce the very best book you can, you will gain support from "opinion molders," and this is very important to your marketing efforts.

Incidentally, it is not necessary to pay peer reviewers. Most are very happy to contribute and are honored to get to see your work before it is printed for general distribution.

Offer to mention them in the Acknowledgments, and send them three free copies when the book comes off the press.

Advise your reviewer to be critical. Their true feelings and thoughts will give you a better opportunity to create the best book you can.

TELL PEERS

A review of your book by people in your field will help bring to light any major problems and give you the assurance that your work is complete. Your peer review will reveal whether or not your information is correct and complete.

The peer review is important even if you are writing fiction. There may be situations or settings based on historical fact or technical processes. Have someone with an extensive background in that area review that part of your manuscript. And it is always desirable to have another writer critique your style.

Incorporate the experts' ideas in the third draft. Make changes in the manuscript using those comments. Weigh each suggestion. An expert may have a valid point, or he or she may have misunderstood what you were trying to convey. In either case, a change is in order.

ASK FRIENDS TO PROOFREAD a copy of your manuscript for grammar, punctuation, readability, clarity and content. Have them pencil their comments right on the pages. Do they find the book easy to read? Do they understand what you are saying? If they do not have time to read the whole book, ask them to go over an interesting chapter.

Be careful whom you pick. You want someone who will be sympathetic to your project but who can also be objective. Do not select someone opposed to your point of view. For example, do not ask a fly fisherman to review your book on bait fishing.

The most valuable of all talents is that of never using two words when one will do. — Thomas Jefferson

Fourth draft: copy edit. Edit for copy flow and punctuation. While you probably skipped around from chapter to chapter in the first, second and third drafts, start this editing process from the beginning. Go through the manuscript one section at a time and concentrate on grammar, spelling and punctuation. Try to edit the whole book in just a few days in order to keep the entire manuscript in mind. This makes it easier to spot any inconsistencies, redundancies or holes in your coverage.

If you are selling your manuscript to a traditional publishing house, they will re-edit it. Publishers have "sponsoring editors" who read manuscripts, recommend their purchase and follow them through to production as well as "copyeditors" who polish manuscripts. In small houses, the sponsoring and copyeditor may be the same person.

4TH EDIT

11

THE END IS IN SIGHT
Finishing the Manuscript

W HEN TO CONSIDER YOUR BOOK FINISHED. If the book is 100 percent accurate and 99 percent complete, go to press. That one last photo and that one extra item can wait for the revised edition. Waiting for one more piece can go on forever. If you delay the publishing, you may miss the market.

THE PROPER LENGTH OF A MANUSCRIPT is precisely what you need to cover the topic completely without being wordy or redundant. Many people feel 128 pages is a minimum and 256 might be a maximum. Some books are too long.

Nonfiction books are not just words. They may have illustrations, tables, resources, blank pages or other supplementary material. Make sure the book has enough "heft" to be considered a book but not so many pages that it becomes expensive to produce and threatening to the reader.

Many publishers still want the finished manuscript to be laser printed, double-spaced on one side of 8½" x 11" white paper.

Start each chapter about one-third of the way from the top of the page and make it appear just as you want it in the book by listing the chapter number and title. At the top of each page, type your name and the chapter/page number. Leave about a one-inch margin all around the page so you and the editor will have room for penciling in notes.

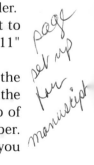
page set up for manuscript

PROOFREADER'S MARKS are standardized to enable you to communicate clearly with your editor, typesetter and printer. A complete set of marks can be found in your dictionary under "proofreader's marks." Stick to the standard marks. If you make up your own, you will only confuse those who must understand them. Use these marks throughout the editing/proofreading process.

ARTWORK. Illustrations consist of line work and halftones. Line work is a clean black-on-white drawing without any shading. Line drawings may be pasted directly onto the boards unless their size must be enlarged or reduced. Halftones are made from photographs, or drawings with shading, by taking a photograph of them through a screen. You will notice the result by looking at a printed photograph through a magnifying glass. A screened photograph is composed of many tiny dots of various sizes (shading).

If you need line work and cannot draw, you can hire a commercial artist. Most typesetters have illustrators on their staffs or know some. These artists usually work inexpensively. See the collaboration chapter for a discussion of hiring and paying illustrators.

Your layout artist or printer may also have a large file or discs of "clip art," and you may find something there you can use. Clip art drawings are provided commercially on a large variety of subjects that may be used without further copyright permission. However, most clip art seems dated. Many people lift art from reprints of old Sears catalogs and other publications where the copyright has expired. Depending on your subject, you may find useful drawings in certain military and government publications that are in the public domain.

PHOTOS AND DRAWINGS are easily indicated in the manuscript with page and position numbers. The second photo on page 40 of Chapter Three would be marked "3-40-B," for example. Mark the location both in the manuscript and on the back of the photo or drawing. Mark the photo near its edge and do not press too hard, you may push through and damage the photo. Incidentally, it is sometimes necessary to indicate which side of the photo goes up if it is not obvious to someone unfamiliar with the subject. Type the captions into the manuscript under the photo position number. Make photocopies of the photos or contact prints and paste them into the manuscript (set the copy machine on "light"). This will make the manuscript clearer both to you and to those who edit or proof for you. Never paste in the photos themselves; they are hard to get off and may be damaged.

PHOTOGRAPHS, rarely seen in fiction, are almost a requirement in nonfiction, especially in how-to books. The most successful how-to books are those that integrate words and pictures to form an attractive teaching tool. Unless you are writing an art-type book, you will use black and white rather than the more expensive color. Color requires four trips through the press plus pre-press "color separations." The best photos are large (they become sharper when reduced), glossy black and whites with a lot of contrast. Color photos and slides may be reproduced in black and white, but they may appear somewhat muddy. Photographs which have already been printed once may be pasted in directly or reduced and re-screened, but the results are not as good as with an original glossy photo. When in doubt about the suitability of a photo, ask a printer. Occasionally the screening actually improves the photo.

USING THE CAMERA. As you compile your manuscript, make a photo list so you will know what pictures you need. Then set out with your gear to take them. Try to include only the object, person or activity you are trying to show; avoid distracting clutter. For good contrast, avoid tonal shades.

Put people in your photos. If you are showing a number of pieces of clothing which are better modeled, invite as many different people as possible to wear them. You can bet that each model will buy a copy of the book. When taking still shots of people, make them smile. Get their teeth in the picture. Most people do not know how to pose for a photo and complain that they do not photograph well. Catch them smiling and they will love you for it. Try to capture action in your photos, make them move. Seek the unusual, tell a story, look for human interest, shoot from a different angle. Then have your film processed by a custom photo lab. Do not send it out through your supermarket. Slides do not matter as much, but in black and white processing the enlarger must be carefully and precisely focused.

Photographs slated for screening and printed reproduction should have more contrast. Tell the photo processor that the photos are "for reproduction." The resulting photographic prints will appear slightly harsh.

Handle negatives and photos carefully; you have a lot invested in them. Keep them clean and mail them flat between cardboard sheets.

When you want the typesetter or printer to crop a print, do not take out the scissors; make crop marks on the edges of the photographic print. If a photo needs retouching (to remove an extraneous object like your camera bag, for example), let the graphic artist do it. Do not use paper clips. For more information on cameras and photography, see the discussion in *Writer's Market*.

Photo release forms are advisable, particularly for pictures of minors. Permission might cost $20-$500, but normally your subjects are just tickled to be in the book. A news photo usually does not require a release unless it is used in an advertisement. A release form may consist of a simple statement giving permission to use a photo in return for a stated amount of money.

OTHER PHOTO SOURCES. Freelancers with a stock of photos will sell them in quantity for a negotiable fee. Or you can have them custom shot. Photo shoots can run $400 to $600 per day plus expenses such as travel and developing and printing costs. When dealing with professional photographers, get prices in advance. Prices will vary greatly with experience.

The chamber of commerce, private firms, trade associations and some governmental agencies have public relations departments that provide photos as part of their function. Libraries and museums sometimes have photo files but museums often charge for the photographs and restrict you to a one-time use. If you publish a second printing, they get another use fee.

Stock photo agencies are in the business of selling pre-shot photos. Some are The Image Bank (2400 Broadway, #220, Santa Monica, CA 90403), and the Corbis-Bettmann Archive (902 Broadway, New York, NY 10010), and Photo Researchers (60 East 56th Street, New York, NY 10022). Agencies belonging to the American Society of Magazine Publishers charge royalties of about $125 for one-time use of a half-page black-and-white photo.

Royalty-free photos are available on CD ROMs. Prices for these disks run from $25 to $250. For information about stock photos on the Internet, check out PhotoSource International (http://www.photosource.com), the largest Website for stock photographers and photobuyers, offering 58 information and service sections. Photo editors and researchers can search by subject matter in a text only version of a directory that lists descriptions of photos by photographers and their specialty areas. There are also newsletters on the site that help photo editors, researchers, photographers and photo buyers keep pace with what's happening in the stock photo industry.

The Library of Congress has a vast collection of historical photographs and will make prints for you if they have the negative. For a catalog, write to the Library of Congress, Prints and Photographs Division, Washington, DC 20540-4730. Or browse their Prints and Photographs Reading Room on-line at: http://lcweb.loc.gov/rr/print. Also see the National Archives (Ninth & Constitution) and the Smithsonian Institution, in Washington, DC. Picture sources are listed in *Writer's Market* and *Literary Market Place*.

Photos from old books with expired copyrights are easily copied with your camera. Just carry the book over to the light, lay it out flat and snap a photo. These photos of photos come out very nicely.

When covering an event, make contact with the other photographers and get their business cards. They may have just what you need.

MAILING THE MANUSCRIPT. The big day has arrived. You will be sending your manuscript off either to your publisher or, if self-publishing, to your printer. If your publisher or printer is not nearby, you will have to ship the manuscript. Stack the photos and drawings and enclose them in cardboard to avoid bending. Enclose both manuscript and illustrations in plastic bags and pack them in a sturdy cardboard carton. The post office does offer a special manuscript rate (same as book rate), but most authors prefer United Parcel Service or Fed Ex because the service is good and the parcel must be signed for on the receiving end. A couple of extra dollars now is well worth the expense. Be sure the carton contains your complete return address.

Always keep a copy of the manuscript. The best way to do this is to keep both a hard copy and a disk. This is to protect you in case the original is lost in the mail or by the printer. And it is your ready reference when the publisher or layout artist calls with questions. Take the manuscript to a copy center. They usually give reduced rates for overnight service and are reasonably inexpensive.

Writing a book is a manageable project if you have a system. With the organization outlined here, your decision to go and a little discipline, you can start a whole new rewarding life.

It is hard to be good at what you do—even harder to be great. But when the job is finished and the results are better than anyone expected, there's a feeling of pride that wells up inside you and makes it all worthwhile.

12

HOW DO YOU AUTHOR A BOOK WHEN YOU CAN'T WRITE?

There is a difference between being an *author* and being a *writer*. An author creates material, while a writer commits material to paper. There are many authors with a lifetime of experience and there are many very good writers who do not have the experience or expertise required to produce a book-length manuscript. The solution is to introduce these two types of people. Combining the knowledge of the expert/creator with the talent and training of the professional writer makes the odds of producing a superior product very favorable. Some people cannot write because they:

- Do not have enough time
- Do not like to write
- Consider themselves idea people
- Do not have the patience
- Do not have the training to be polished writers
- Cannot make the emotional commitment to this type of solitude and perseverance

Lee Iacocca, like other celebrities, did not write his two bestsellers all by himself; he had two different writers. And it was announced in 1998 that basketball star Shaquille O'Neal was "writing" a children's book for Scholastic, Inc. The title: *Shaq and the Beanstalk.*

If you cannot afford to take time from your career to become an expert writer, it may be more practical and cost-effective to leave the writing of the manuscript to a writing professional. If, for example, your "other" work pays you $100 per hour, it does not make economic sense to spend time doing work you can buy for $25. You may decide to hire a keyboarder, editor, co-author, ghostwriter or other collaborator.

au'thŏr, *n.* [ME. *autour*; OFr. *autor*; L. *auctor*, author, from *augere*, to cause to grow, increase.]
  1. one who produces, creates, or brings into being; the beginner, creator, or first mover of anything.
  2. one who composes or writes a book, or whose occupation is to compose and write books.

wrīt'ẽr, *n.* 1. one who writes, has written, or is in the habit of writing.
  2. a person whose business or occupation is writing; specifically, (a) a copyist; a scribe or clerk; (b) an author, journalist, or the like.

With permission. From *Webster's New Twentieth Century Dictionary*, Second Edition. Copyright © 1983 by Simon & Schuster, Inc.

TEAM APPROACH. Behind most authors is a small army of support troops. They may be content editors, copyeditors, technical editors, readers, researchers, indexers, proofreaders, literary scouts, agents, librarians, publisher's representatives, translators or anyone else who offers a service connected with book writing. You have to decide what kind of help you need and what you can afford. To help you, we will relate some actual partnership stories.

Jim Comiskey is a successful businessman who does not type. When he decided to author a book, he took a strictly-business approach and paid for the help he needed. He read up on his subject, conducted interviews, researched the topic and made an outline. Then he hand-wrote the first draft. After reviewing and editing his writing, he dictated the manuscript for How to Start, Expand & Sell a Business *into a tape recorder and sent it to a word processing service. He located the service through a local university by asking for a "thesis typist." His slow speech allowed the typists to type straight off the tape recorder; they did not even need a dictating machine with foot pedal.*

Jim edited the hard-copy printout and gave it back to the service for entering. The cost was $15 per hour and, even with many revisions, amounted to only $1,800. Then he sent a clean version to a professional editor to check punctuation and grammar. This editor was found through a local writers' group and the thorough editing cost $1,000.

Once again, the manuscript was returned to the word processing service to enter the corrections. The floppy disk was sent to a typesetter to avoid more keyboarding and proofing. The typesetter charged $1,500 to set the type and to paste up the 8½" x 11", 265-page book.

Jim paid $1,000 for the cover art. He found the artist through a listing in Literary Market Place. *Because he dictated his book, Jim did not have to learn to type or improve his handwriting. Because he relied on professional editors, he did not have to learn punctuation or grammar. The result is an original book in a conversational style. It received excellent reviews. By the way, costs listed here may be higher today in your area.*

DICTATING. If you cannot type, try dictation. If you can speak in a logical, informative fashion, you can dictate for transcribing; get a tape recorder. Do the transcriptions yourself or hire a secretary. Then edit the hard copy and either correct the language or leave it as is. Sometimes a basic speaking style adds to the book.

I love being a writer. What I can't stand is the paperwork.
— Peter DeVries

When dictating, you need an outline and notes if you want the manuscript to flow in any sort of order. Dictation will help you get your message on paper, but you still need to be organized.

Barbara Cartland, the queen of romantic novels (over 350 million copies of her books are in print), dictates her novels to a secretary. So far she has authored more than 200 books this way. One year, working between 1:00 p.m. and 3:30 p.m., she talked out twenty-two books at the rate of 6-7,000 words (one chapter) per day. Now 88, she still "writes" up to 30,000 words a week. Cartland dreams up the plot, follows the romance formula and then lets the story flow in her famous storytelling style.

WHEN YOU DON'T HAVE THE TIME TO WRITE. Many people today have tremendous ideas, a great store of information, and creative approaches. But they are so busy they do not have time to write a book. These people need collaborators.

Mindy Bingham is an organizer, an idea person and a doer whose creative mind never shuts off, but she moves too fast to polish her writing and she does not dwell on proper spelling. Mindy took the Girls Club of Santa Barbara in financial crisis, turned it around and made the service organization a financial success by authoring and producing a book on the Club's behalf. She envisioned a book for teenage girls on self-awareness and personal planning. She roughed it out incorporating the exercises and questionnaires she had developed, had Judy Edmondson research and write other parts and then shipped the whole manuscript off to Sandy Stryker in Los Angeles. Sandy, a former newspaper reporter and now an advertising copywriter, rewrote the book contributing flow, continuity, style and zip. The book, recognized as a classic in its field, would never have come about if these three women with diverse talents had not come together as a team.

COLLABORATION is often the marriage of an expert/author who does not have the time or ability to write and a writer without original material. Or, it may be a co-authorship of experts in like or dissimilar fields. Which of the following types of collaboration would work best for you?

CO-AUTHORSHIP involves two or more people. Often all participants are recognized experts. Ideally, they are also equally competent writers, but this is a rare occurrence indeed. They may contribute equally to the workload, or one partner may carry a heavier burden. Probably the person with the most recognized name will do less of the actual writing, but more of the content editing.

Gordon Burgett is an author-publisher who spends a good part of the year traveling the California State University circuit teaching classes on writing, publishing, speaking and how to give seminars. Mike Frank is a well-known professional speaker. Gordon's writing is technically excellent and he is a great speaker, but Mike is better known in speaking circles. The two joined together to produce the manuscript Speaking For Money. *Each wrote in his area of expertise and then Burgett did the rewriting, editing and publishing.*

Dan Poynter shared the responsibilities for the Frisbee Players' Handbook *with disc champion Mark Danna. Danna wrote the throwing and catching chapters, while Poynter wrote on history, record attempts and competition and also assembled the appendix. While Poynter came up with the unique package and marketing idea, he did not have enough expertise or credibility as a Frisbee player to produce a book that would be taken seriously. Mark Danna rounded out the team well.*

If you have a book you want to do yourself but recognize that you lack the required technical expertise, consider co-authorship. Find an expert in the field to write the technical part while you write the other part and then each of you can edit the other's material. This approach has many advantages, including the endorsement of an expert, credibility and someone else to send on the promotional tour. The disadvantages are smaller royalties, extra accounting and author handholding.

A doctor, who is also an excellent writer (and who asked that his name not be used), collaborated with another doctor who was a nationally recognized expert in a new surgical technique. The writer-doctor did most of the actual work, while the doctor with the name in the field did final editing and lent his name to the work. Though the workload was unequal, the doctors shared the royalties equally. And, as a result of the book, the writer-doctor made a name for himself in a new and exciting field.

THE EXPERT/WRITER TEAM can be successful even if the writer joins the project knowing nothing about the proposed subject. It is the expert's responsibility to provide the research, data, and experience that will make the book valuable. When two people collaborate in this manner, it may seem that the writer is doing more work because he or she is spending more time on the project than the expert. The writer must remember that a lot of the expert's work was done long before the writer came into the project. The expert has spent years perfecting and increasing his or her knowledge. Be sure to discuss who will do what and how much at the beginning of the collaboration process to avoid hard feelings later on. Use the responsibility chart in Chapter Thirteen to clarify roles.

Writing is no trouble: you just jot down ideas as they occur to you. The jotting is simplicity itself—it is the occurring which is difficult. — Stephen Leacock

SPOUSES AS WRITING PARTNERS. The first place to look for a writing partner is your spouse. Maybe you have one of those relationships where opposites attract. One of you is detail and research-oriented, while the other has a creative mind that never shuts off. If at least one of you is a competent writer, why not team up on your book?

Sit down together and go over the five T's in Chapter Two. If between the two of you, you can answer most of the questions in the affirmative, you have the makings of a great writing partnership.

Teresa and Raf Dahlquist teamed up for a series of books. Together, they developed a charming line of whimsically illustrated children's stories about famous scientists. Their first was Mr. Halley and His Comet. Raf is a highly technical scientist who does the research, while Teresa is the idea person who writes the prose.

Even if one spouse has no experience outside the home a project like this gets both of them published, provides them with a common project (which may do great things for the marriage) and elevates their job status.

WRITING BY COMMITTEE. Committees write many textbooks. If two heads are better than one, does it hold true that three, four or five are better still? It can. But as the number of authors moves from two to three or more, it becomes more difficult to keep the manuscript tight, the communication clear and the workloads equal while still allowing some creativity to filter in. The committee members must remember that they are a team. They must work up a game plan that will outline everyone's responsibilities clearly, diagram the decision-making process and provide deadlines. In Chapter Thirteen you will find responsibility and decision-making charts that can help clarify responsibilities, avoid conflict and eliminate duplication of effort.

There is nothing wrong with writing poorly, but there is no excuse for not having it cleaned up by an editor.

GHOSTWRITERS write for money not for fame—their names do not go on the cover of the book. How many ghostwriters do you know? Would you know one if you saw one? Ghostwriters, by definition, are invisible. They write your book for you from your notes and thoughts.

These writers usually deal in autobiography. Most celebrity books are ghosted. Ghosts often obtain information through interviews (both the "author" and everyone around him or her) and then flesh out the material and commit it to paper. This interviewing may take quite a bit of time because the ghost has to get to know the author well. The drafts are returned to the "author" for content editing and are then rewritten by the invisible collaborator.

Ghostwriting a book can take as much as two years, so it can be costly. If you are famous, ghosts will often write for 50 percent of the advance and royalties because they know the book will be published by a major publisher. If you are not famous, you will normally pay the ghost a flat fee. Fees run from $10,000 to $35,000 depending on the size and complexity of the book but $65,000 is not unheard of. Those who get a percentage may do a better job as they care more about the success of the book. This kind of collaboration costs more than editing or co-authoring because ghosts do a greater amount of the work.

Ghosts should get some credit in the book. A cover credit could read ". . . as told to Sid Smith." " . . . with Sid Smith" or "Edited by Sid Smith." A ghostwriter may be mentioned in the acknowledgments or the copyright page may contain a statement such as "Packaged and produced by Carolyn Porter." Or "And Special Thanks to Carolyn Porter."

Poets and fiction writers sometimes turn to ghosting to buy time for their own work. Many find it to be good practice.

The man of science appears to be the only man who has something to say just now—and the only man who does not know how to say it. — Sir James Barrie

CONTRACT WRITING requires even less "author" input than ghosting. Often the author provides only the subject, some unique ideas and an indication of the direction the project should follow. Contracted books are often wrapped up in less than 60 days by moonlighting advertising copywriters or journalists. Many nonfiction books, other than autobiographies, are contracted. These books might be company histories, manuals for a new product or how-to books.

Back in the seventies, Joe Karbo was famous for his Lazy Man's Way to Riches. *His full-page ads featuring small type and large hype started a new trend in advertising copywriting. Even after he passed away, the modest book continued to sell at $10 a copy—for a total of over nine million dollars so far. The untold story is that Joe paid to have his idea written. His investment was less than $3,000.*

Many of the more successful book houses approach publishing from a hard-nosed marketing position. They know what they have been able to sell in the past and they stay in their field of expertise, often by assigning writers to produce more of these "contracted books." Magazine editors have always relied on freelancers, so buying the material from others is not new or unusual.

Once you have decided on an area of concentration, you, too, may approach others to write for you by paying cash outright or using modest royalty advances as an inducement. The accounting is easier and the arrangement is often more cost-effective if you pay outright for the help you need. Minimum flat fees are often around $5,000 to $10,000 for a short book (150 to 250 pages), half to be paid on assignment and half on acceptance of a complete manuscript. Contracted writers should be paid on a schedule. They usually do not share in the copyright and generally do not receive editorial control over the work. The writer sells his or her labor and has no further claim to it.

In a ghosted book, the writer is using the author as the main resource. In a contracted book, the manuscript is assembled mostly from research. Ghostwriting usually takes longer and is more complex.

EDITORS. Perhaps you can get your thoughts down on paper but all that good information does not read very well. What you need is an editor, someone who can take your information and clean it up.

Editors may be the basic copyeditors who dot "i's" and cross "t's," or they may be rewrite editors who add zip to your writing: energy, order and clarity.

A professional editing job can make a major difference in manuscript success and acceptability. If you do not have a strong journalistic background, editors are a good investment.

Lost time is never found again. — Benjamin Franklin

13

FINDING AND WORKING WITH A WRITING PARTNER

If you have decided not to go it alone, here are some tips for finding and working with a collaborator.

WHAT TYPE OF PARTNER DO YOU NEED? Do you need a little light proofreading help? Does your work require major editing? Do you want someone you can work with to get your message down on paper in readable form? Re-evaluate your strengths and limitations by reviewing your author workplan chart in Chapter Two. Do you need a co-author, ghostwriter, contract writer, editor, researcher or keyboarder?

If your book is nonfiction, you want a nonfiction writer, not a poet. The applicant should have a track record; do not hire a novice. Look for someone with experience in writing books, not just short magazine articles.

Draft a job description, establish a work timetable and make up a rough contract. Clarify in your own mind what type of help you need and what you want to have done. Prepare for the interview by having a job description, work schedule and contract drafted.

PREP FOR N.S.

DRAFTING THE JOB DESCRIPTION. Your job description should include the following:

1. Job title
2. Working title of the book

3. Required qualifications for the position
4. What examples of the applicant's work you would like to see
5. A draft of your work timetable
6. How the writer will be credited in the book
7. Duties of the applicant; if hired
8. Salary or remuneration schedule

SAMPLE JOB DESCRIPTION

1. **Job title:** Contract writer.

2. **Title of work:** *The Cat and Dog Handbook.*

3. **Qualifications:** Experienced in the field of nonfiction writing. The ability to research, outline, draft and write an approximately 150-page, 5½" x 8½" book in the area of dog and cat care.

4. **Portfolio** review required. Samples of past work.

5. **Schedule:**
   Contract writer completes research—1/1/___.
   Contract writer completes first draft of book—3/1/___.
   Author completes content edit—3/31/___.
   Contract writer completes second draft—4/30/___.
   Author sends out for peer review to be completed by 6/30/___.
   Contract writer completes third draft—7/15/___.
   Contract writer completes final copy edit and manuscript by 7/30/___.

6. **Contract writer** shall receive co-author status with Author.

7. **Contract writer** shall be responsible for all research, writing and editing of the manuscript. The work will be completed when it is in correct form to be delivered to the typesetter. Contracting Author shall be responsible for providing necessary research direction, content editing of the first draft and locating the peer reviewers for the third draft.

8. **Compensation** shall be paid at the rate of _____. (See discussion.)

WHERE TO FIND A WRITING PARTNER. Start by looking in the *Yellow Pages* under "Writers," "Editorial Services" "Secretarial Services" and "Word Processing Services"; try this right now. Notice how easy it is to find help. Check *Literary Market Place* under "Editorial Services." Here you will find a number of agencies and individuals offering a wide variety of collaborative help.

Typical ads (addresses deleted)

Publishers Weekly, and *Writer's Digest* have classified sections with ads from collaborators. Those who advertise may be more professional.

Contact local writers' groups, editorial services and secretarial services through local bookstores and libraries. They know the people in the writing profession in your locale. Be a detective, ask for recommendations and follow each lead. Call PR firms or advertising agencies for leads.

If you need research assistance, look for a librarian who wants some moonlighting work. Also try the local college, where you will find students happy to work at minimum wage. The lucky student may even be able to obtain college credit while working with you. Credit in your acknowledgments may help them later in their career search, and it also looks good on their resumé. Check the telephone directory and call the student placement office. Of course, you could place your own help-wanted ad.

GHOST WRITER for self-help manuscripts. Living money, royalties. Executive Reno home. Travel. Prefer female to age 45.

Wanted: Experienced writer. Expand corporate intrigue and dialogue. Condensed novel. Material recognized world wide. Potential block buster. Will split %. Resume.

Pro Ghost. Need Ludlum–style writer to complete manuscript. Outline plus 100 pages finished. Top talent a must. Resume, etc.

WANTED: Writer, living in KC area, to work with author on nonfiction book. Write Will

---

Examples of short ads for a ghostwriter

Look for newspaper reporters with some extra time. They are professionals who are used to deadlines. Reporters are trained to listen and to put your thoughts down accurately. Once they have your material written out, you may edit the work. Reporters are also used to having their material edited and do not have too much of their ego tied up in it. The reporter may even wind up doing a feature story on you—and their media contacts are invaluable.

Donald Dible, author-publisher of Up Your Own Organization, *says, "Avoid grade school and high school English teachers. For the most part, they are more concerned with discovering what is wrong with your writing (remember the red ink on your themes?) than in helping you fix it for publication."*

Word of mouth is often the best method for finding help, especially when searching locally. One freelancer will often lead you to others. Writing clubs and other trade associations will usually pass on names, and since they are concerned about their own credibility, you can be reasonably certain the people they recommend will be competent. You should be able to come up with the partner you need. The result should be help for you, work for your partner and a much better book for your readers.

WHAT TO LOOK FOR IN A PARTNER

- **Compatibility.** You must not only get along and work easily with your temporary partner, you must like each other. You will be working very closely in this temporary marriage; you are handing over a segment of your life to this person.

  Make sure the chemistry is right. Does your writer grasp your aims and goals quickly? You should be able to work together so that the result is greater than the sum of the individual contributions. Your partner may do some things better than you—that is what a good partnership is all about. Is there mutual trust? Some people are very protective about what they commit to paper, and editing their work can cause unnecessary strain in the working relationship. Be sure to cover this topic thoroughly in the interview before agreeing to hire the writer.

- **Quality of work.** Your collaborator should have experience in nonfiction book writing if the book is nonfiction or in fiction writing if the book is fiction. Be wary of the person who has never written as a professional. This includes well-meaning instructors of English or journalism as well as the casual journal or magazine writer. Writing is a craft, a profession that requires practice and persistence. If your partner does not approach writing in a businesslike way, you may have problems. You do not need a collaborator who is egocentric, undiplomatic or unreliable.

- **Quantity of work.** If you are hiring an editor, does he or she dot "i's," correct grammar and check spelling? Do you really need a complete rewrite? Evaluate your own writing ability and hire the kind of editor you need. There is a big difference in areas of expertise.

Doctor Hartbrodt wrote a medical book about a common disease. The manuscript contained a lot of solid, helpful information but was hard to read. He contacted writers' groups, editorial services and secretarial services through the Yellow Pages and located four people who were willing to help. He gave each a copy of the first chapter and asked them to edit a couple of sample pages and to quote their fee. Some editors only want to dot "i's", and cross "t's", while others want to do complete rewrites. Using this method, he was able to compare their work and select the one he liked at the best per-page price.

Be very cautious about partnerships. They seem to be so easy to get into and so difficult to get out of.
— Jim Comiskey in *How to Start, Expand & Sell a Business*

- **Compatible work styles**. You and your partner must have the same level of commitment. If one partner is hard-working and can work on past quitting time to get something done right while the other would rather watch the sunset for inspiration, the union is not likely to last.

- **Price**. Fortunately, the supply of writing help is much greater than the demand. Generally, professionals will cost more. You may get a lower price from someone who is not writing full-time. The best advice is to keep interviewing until you find someone you feel comfortable with who is willing to work at a price you can afford.

INTERVIEW QUESTIONS AND PROCESS. Make your first cut over the telephone. Do not waste your time or theirs if there is a reason they should not work for you. Tell callers about your project, your schedule, the proposed length of the manuscript, and so on. In addition, ask them about any specific requirements you might have unrelated to the project. Keep a list of questions by the telephone. They might include:

- What is your experience in writing (or editing, typing, etc.)?
- Do you have experience in the subject?
- Can you meet the time schedule?
- Do you have a car?
- Are you allergic to cats?
- Do you smoke?

If you have a cat, don't want someone smoking in your home and are far from public transportation, save time and take care of these questions now.

Send a copy of your job description to the candidates who pass the initial telephone screening. Use a cover letter to ask them to review the job description and invite them to set up an interview by a given date. This process will save you some time. If your job description is clearly written and complete, the applicant will understand exactly what you want and can make the decision to proceed.

At the interview, have a draft copy of your contract and timetable ready to share with people you think may be finalists. Explain that it is a draft and that some points may be negotiable. When you make your final choice, go over the contract and job description carefully so that all changes can be put in writing before the final agreement is reached.

These potential partners should provide a list of their services, clients they have worked for (references), a resumé and samples of their work. Do not expect a lot of free consulting, though applicants may have some off-the-cuff ideas. Listen to their questions as the best indication of their basic approach, thoroughness and understanding of your situation. Be wary if they betray the confidence of other clients. If they tell on others, they will tell on you.

Follow up on references for finalists. These references should be from people they have worked for in the past in the capacity that you are considering hiring them. Repeat business is the sign of a successful professional writer.

Be sure to check on the following traits when you call references:

1. The ability to take editorial direction
2. The ability to meet deadlines
3. The ability to follow through until completion
4. The quality of their work
5. The candidate's strong points
6. The candidate's weak points

Look for a writer who is businesslike, one who shows up on time with samples and resumés and seems to know what he or she is doing.

The closest to perfection a person ever comes is when he fills out a job application form. — Stanley J. Randall

When hiring an editor, ask each applicant to edit the same sample two to three pages and to submit a per-page quote. If you don't know the work style of the editor, paying by the hour can be dangerously expensive, and you will not want to be standing over anyone with a whip.

A professional will find out your requirements and goals and will help direct your interview session. At the end of the meeting, ask the writer to send you a written quote.

Never hire the first interviewee who walks through the door. Interview ten or more and then select the best one.

PARTNERSHIPS THAT HAPPEN. You might be reading this book because the project you have in mind was conceived by two people. In other words, you already have your partner. These writing partners are usually co-workers or friends. The books they produce often begin over a cup of coffee, at a conference or a social affair when you begin to dream together of a book that is "really needed!" It is often hard to make "partnerships that happen" work. So stop right now and complete the author workplan in Chapter Two. Identify your individual strengths and weaknesses and then work up a plan assigning each of you the most appropriate responsibilities. A workplan will make book authoring a much more rewarding and positive experience for you both.

HOW TO TREAT YOUR PARTNER. Your collaborator is a professional and must be treated fairly. This means paying your partner as agreed, on time. Do not change the parameters of the project without discussion, renegotiations and reduction to writing. Give all the help, background information, time and material he or she needs to do a good job for you.

It was a friendship founded on business, which is a good deal better than a business founded on friendship.
— John D. Rockefeller

Decide how you want to trade material back and forth. Will it be chapter by chapter or manuscript by manuscript? The faster each of you works, the greater the amount of material you can trade. You want to be able to keep the work in mind, so that when the other partner calls, you will know what he or she is talking about.

Clearly establish responsibilities. Each partner must be responsible for specific tasks and have definite deadlines. Projects with two or more partners sometimes fail because certain tasks were left to the "other" partner. Or the work done is redundant.

Communication is very important in a partnership. Time should be set aside periodically to sit down and talk about what is going on, to address new ideas and to improve the project or process. Partners must feel that they can freely state their concerns and that the genuine goal of each person is to create as good a product as possible.

WRITING BY COMMITTEE is where more than two people are contributing to the manuscript. When working with a group there are some important guidelines:

*   One senior author should have final approval power for all manuscript decisions, and this must be understood by all involved before the project begins. The senior author should be someone who can make decisions quickly and comfortably, even when others disagree.
*   The final draft of all work must be written by the same person to achieve a smooth flow and continuity of style.
*   Explicit timetables and responsibilities must be negotiated, agreed to and adhered to.

I've always believed in writing without a collaborator, because where two people are writing the same book, each believes he gets all the worries and only half the royalties.
— Agatha Christie

- Regular meetings must be held at predetermined times with written agendas and with commitments to attend by all involved.

- There must be a termination clause in the contract in case one member decides to leave or is unable to fulfill his or her commitment. A termination clause tells all concerned what the alternative is to completing the project and sets out the process for removing someone from the work.

RESPONSIBILITY AND DECISION-MAKING CHARTS. On whatever basis you hire help or work with partners, you must agree in advance on how you plan to divide the work. Each of you must know and understand the limits and obligations the agreement imposes on you both. One way is to develop an outline and then assign responsibility with deadlines to each part of the project. The timetable must be realistic.

Here is a responsibility chart for two co-authors that are writing a nonfiction book on how to open a boutique. Wendy is the expert/idea person and Nancy is a professional writer who works as a newspaper reporter. Neither of them feels totally competent to do the final copyedit on the book, so they have decided to hire a copyeditor. This chart provides a clear map showing how and when the tasks will be completed.

RESPONSIBILITY CHART FOR BOUTIQUE BUSINESS BOOK (TWO PEOPLE)

Task	Wendy	Nancy	Projected completion date
PREPARATION			
Set up binder	R		1/30/__
Gather all books and magazines	R		2/15/__
Write for information	R		2/1/__
Write outline of book	R		3/1/__
Organize in "pilot system"	R		3/15/__
FIRST DRAFT			
Outline each chapter	R		4/30/__
Complete first draft		R	7/30/__
SECOND DRAFT			
Review for gaps	R		8/__
Research to fill gaps	R		8/30/__
Edit first draft	R		9/15/__
Complete second draft		R	10/15/__
List needed photos and drawings	R		9/30/__
THIRD DRAFT			
Locate peer reviewers	R		10/1/__
Manage manuscript transfers	R		10/15/__
Edit peer notes	R		11/15/__
Complete third draft		R	12/1/__

Task	Wendy	Nancy	Projected completion date
FOURTH DRAFT			
Hire copyeditor	R		11/15/__
Enter changes and prepare final manuscript	R		12/30/__
MANUSCRIPT FINALIZATION			
Write for permissions	R		12/30/__
Footnotes		R	12/30/__
Bibliography		R	12/30/__
Appendix		R	12/30/__
Table of contents		R	12/30/__
Send ABI and for LC	R		12/30/__
Final check on statistics		R	12/30/__
See that clean copy is complete		R	1/1/__
Send printed book for copyright	R		

The following decision-making chart outlines the tasks, responsibilities and communication structure for a committee of college professors working on a textbook. Decision making within a group of three or more people can become very cumbersome. What happens is either too much time is spent polling the committee on how members feel a task should be handled or not enough input is received from committee members and they feel their ideas and opinions are not valued. In either case, tension is created and valuable energy and time are diverted. That time and energy should go into manuscript production. Developing a decision-making chart in the beginning will help eliminate frustration later on.

RESPONSIBILITY AND DECISION MAKING CHART
For committee working on a college textbook
for entrepreneurial course

Codes:

A = This person has final approval. He or she may veto a
project or direction.

R = This person is responsible for initiating a task and seeing it
through to completion.

C = This person wants to be consulted before a decision is
made on a task but has no veto power.

I = This person needs to be informed on what the final
decision is but does not have to be consulted.

Task	Author A	Author B	Author C	Author D	Completion date
Complete chapter order	R	C	C	C	1/30/__
Outline of the book	R	C	C	C	3/11/__
Complete research and draft appropriate chapters in the areas of: Evaluating your motives		R			6/1/__
Researching your industry		R			7/15/__
Business Finance	R		C		6/1/__
Market Research	C		R		6/1/__
Writing your Business Plan		C		R	6/1/__
Attracting Investors		C		R	7/15/__
Partnerships		R		C	9/1/__
Personnel	C		R		9/1/__

Task	Author A	Author B	Author C	Author D	Completion date
The future of entrepreneurial-ship	R				7/15/__
Content editing of total manuscript	R				9/2/__
Locate peer reviewers and facilitate review process		R	R	I	6/1/__
Write for permissions	I		R		10/1/__
Completion of index	I	R			10/1/__
Negotiate contract with publisher	A	C	R	C	6/1/__
Accuracy of footnotes	I		R		10/1/__
Responsible for total rewrite of the manuscript	A			R	10/15/__
Copyediting for spelling and grammar				R	11/15/__
Responsible for producing final clean copy	A			R	12/1/__
Monitor of decision-making chart	A				
Call meetings of authors	R				monthly
Name the book	A	C	C	C	11/1/__
List of resources for photos	A		R		11/1/__

DECISION MAKING CHART

A sample decision-making chart for a cookbook written by a committee of community volunteers for their favorite charity

Task	Committee chair	Author B	Author C	Author D	Author E	Completion date
Outline the book with chapter headings	A	R	C	C	C	2/1/__
Design recipes, submission form and procedures	A	C	R	C	I	1/15/__
Solicit collaborators and volunteers to submit recipes	R	R	R	R	R	5/1/__
Review, test and edit recipes submitted and research any others in the areas of: Hors d'oeuvres, drinks and snacks	A	R				
Main dishes and meats	A		R			
Desserts and pastry section	A			R		
Salads and vegetables	A				R	
Submit draft of each cookbook section	A	R	R	R	R	8/1/__
Rewrite first draft for continuity of style	A			R		10/1/__
Content edit	R	C	C	C	C	11/1/__
Copyedit					R	11/15/__
Prepare final copy of corrected manuscript	A				R	12/1/__
Finalize title	A	C	C	C	C	12/1/__
Decide how to publish the book and conduct necessary negotiations	R	C	C	I	I	12/1/__

A FEW FINAL NOTES ON AUTHORING PARTNERSHIPS.
Teamwork is the key to a good relationship. Avoid the
adversary attitude. A good partnership, like a good marriage,
can be exciting and very productive. Two people bouncing
ideas off one another can create a much better product.

Each partner must contribute 100 percent to the project
every time he or she works on the manuscript. Do not leave
rough edges for the other partner to clean up. If you want the
example changed, write it, or at least rough it out, yourself.
Do not write "change example." "Correcting" or directing the
partner does not foster a close working relationship. If you
want something in the manuscript, put it in.

It is important to realize there will be certain sentences,
sections or editorial comments that are sacred to the other
partner. If you are writing back and forth, editing each other's
work, and the originator of the material finds a sacred part
deleted, changed or edited, tempers may flare. Establish a
communication technique to anticipate this situation. One
possibility would be to establish that the word sacred used in
the margin means that any editing of that part must be done
as a joint venture in a formal meeting. Obviously, the word
"sacred" should not be used too often or the writing and
editing process will get bogged down.

When critiquing your partner's work, be sensitive in how
you phrase your comments and the approach you take!

Collaborative book writing often takes much longer than
going it alone. The procedure is slowed because of the joint
editing, rewriting and meetings. This is typical committee
work. But the trade-off may produce a better product.

---

*No passion in the world is equal to the passion to alter
someone else's draft.* — H.G. Wells

COLLABORATORS
"FAIR FIGHTING" RULES

- Criticize a specific sentence or paragraph, not the other person.
- When discussing a problem area, always finish your observation with ... "a better way might be. ...".
- Begin a critique with a positive observation. "What I like is .... "What I think needs work is. ...."
- Take turns being the "critic" (devil's advocate).
- Listen to the other person's point of view and be able to restate that view before you react.
- Follow the decision with a wink, smile, hug or kiss (depending on your relationship).

AND explain to your children (and/or others around you) that you are critically discussing the project, not disagreeing with each other.

With a good collaborator you find that two heads are, indeed, better than one. — Raymond Hull in *How to Write How-to Books and Articles*

14

NEGOTIATING AND CONTRACTING WITH COLLABORATORS

Signing a contract with your collaborator may seem excessively businesslike—as though you do not trust each other. If your collaborator is a close friend or spouse, you may be tempted to skip this chapter altogether. Don't! Written agreements are often more important when people are close.

The object of a writing contract is to clarify the thinking and positions of both parties while arriving at a mutually beneficial agreement. You and your collaborator will be working together closely for a long time, so both of you have to feel the agreement is consistent and fair.

First-time writers will be eager to become published and may not be terribly concerned about the contract—initially. Many creative people are not business or commercially oriented. It is imperative that contract negotiation and signing be taken care of before the writing begins. Write a rough draft of the contract and ask your potential partner whether it is generally acceptable. Remember that people who write contracts slant them their way. You have an advantage if you draft the contract rather than accept a contract written by the other party. Here is a sample contract with a discussion of some of the items to be considered when an author (you) contracts with a writer.

A verbal contract isn't worth the paper it's printed on.
— Samuel Goldwyn, founder of MGM

CONTRACT WRITER WORK AGREEMENT. If your collaboration is with a contract writer or ghost, use this contract writer agreement and alter it to fit your situation. This draft will save time by helping you to clarify your own thinking. Then take it to a contract attorney who is familiar with copyright law and book publishing. Most lawyers work by the hour, and editing your contract will take less time than starting from scratch.

DRAFT OF A CONTRACT WRITER AGREEMENT

This agreement is made between _____ (the Writer) and _____ (the Author).

It is agreed that Writer is to write for Author a book approximately _____ words in length, provisionally titled _____.

It is agreed that the Author will supply all information that the Writer may require to complete the book.

The text and credits are to be framed so as to give the Author full and sole credit as author of the book. Writer agrees to keep the nature of Writer's contribution and the fact that the book will be published under the name of Author, strictly confidential.

If, for the preparation of illustrations for the book, it is necessary to engage artists or photographers, the costs of such work are to be borne entirely by the Author. Otherwise, the entire work and cost of preparing a manuscript fit for publishing, such as research, typing and photocopying, shall be undertaken by the Writer.

Writer is responsible for securing any copyright clearances.

The responsibility of reading and correcting proofs and compiling an index shall be undertaken by the Writer.

The copyright for the finished work is to be held solely by the Author; all royalties resulting from the sale of the book, or from the sale of subsidiary rights, are to go to the Author

Writer agrees not to use information gained during the preparation of this work to write any competitive work on the same or any allied subject.

Writer acknowledges that all confidential ideas for the book have been supplied by Author and are the exclusive property of Author. Writer acknowledges access to certain of Author's trade secrets.

Writer shall be responsible only for writing a manuscript fit for submission to publishers. The work and expense of finding a market for it shall be undertaken by Author.

Writer shall submit a manuscript which is satisfactory to Author in form and content. Acceptability of the written work shall be at the sole discretion of Author. Work may be stopped at any time by Author.

Work timetable: (See example in Chapter Seven.)

Fees. For completing the manuscript, in form fit for submission to publishers, Author will pay Writer the total sum of _____ dollars. The manner of payment shall be as follows:

1. On completion of this agreement, and before commencement of the work, an advance of _____ dollars.

2. On completion of the first draft, _____ dollars.

3. On completion of the second draft, _____ dollars.

4. On completion of the final draft, _____ dollars.

5. On completion of proofreading and indexing, _____ dollars.

6. And any previously approved, mutually agreed upon expenses.

These fees are full and complete and Writer fully understands there will be no further compensation or royalties.

This is a work for hire in which Author owns all copyright interests, and Writer assigns all of same to Author.

This contract shall run for the copyright life of the book and is binding on Author's and Writer's heirs, successors and assigns.

This contract is being entered into in good faith. It is the only agreement for this book between Author and Writer.

(signed)

Author: _____

Writer: _____

Date: _____

Use this contract as a guide and consult your legal advisor.

If your collaboration is between two, more or less, equal partners (e.g., co-authors), use the work agreement as an outline to make sure you have addressed all the important issues in your contract. Now let's discuss some of the items mentioned in the draft agreement.

CREDITS OR BILLING. How will the authorship of this book be listed on the cover and in all the book directories? Is your collaborator a true co-author or a ghost?

The courts are full of people litigating verbal agreements. People have very selective memories when partnership trouble starts. — Jim Comiskey in *How to Start, Expand & Sell a Business*

Allison Author

Allison Author with the assistance of Wendell Writer

Allison Author as told to Wendell Writer

Allison Author with Wendell Writer

Allison Author and Wendell Writer

Wendell Writer and Allison Author

There is no hard and fast rule on cover billing, but a lot depends on who is contributing what and how much to the product. Generally, your writer should get either billing or money. Ghostwriters usually do not receive name credit as they are supposed to be invisible. If you are paying top dollar, you are buying the billing for yourself. If the writer wants his or her name on the cover, the paycheck should be lower.

If this is simply a marriage between an expert who can't write and a writer without a book idea, turn this apparent weakness into an asset by listing each person's qualifications in the book credits and describe the union as the perfect marriage.

FLAT FEES OR ROYALTIES. Should contributors get a percentage of the book or be paid a flat fee? Obviously, flat fees are simpler and occasionally cheaper. Generally, a person creating a major portion of the book should get royalties, while someone doing basic research, typing or contributing a drawing should be paid a set fee.

If you require a few drawings, go to a graphic artist and have them drawn to order. Then pay the bill and be done with it. The artist deserves a piece of the action no more than the person who painted your car before you sold it. Children's picture books require extensive illustrations, so the artist usually splits the royalties with the author.

If you hire an artist to make a major contribution to your book, obtain a written release and assignment of any copyright interest he or she might have. Many authors negotiate a lower price for art by buying the right to use it in their book (present and future editions) only. The artist is free to peddle the illustrations elsewhere outside the book trade. The same is true for photographs.

DRAFT ARTIST RELEASE

This is to confirm the understanding that I, _____ , have (taken photographs, provided artwork, etc.) for a book tentatively titled _____ by _____ (Author).

All rights in and to the (photographs or artwork), including the copyright and renewal and extension of copyright on these (photographs or artwork) shall belong to Author, and I assign all said copyright interests to Author. My contributions are works for hire in which I retain no copyright interest.

Author shall have the right to use my name in sales promotion or advertising of the work.

Name: _____

Witness: _____

Date: _____

80/20?

Co-authors usually split advances and royalties based on their predicted contributions to the manuscript. Expert/ writer teams either split royalties or the writer receives a flat fee. Ghosts will write a book for $5,000 to $35,000 and up. But, if you are famous and the book is to be sold to a publisher, the ghost may perceive it to be in his or her interest to ask for up to 50 percent of what the book earns. If you plan to self-publish, or the sales are not projected to be too great, the ghost may want a flat fee. Royalty reports are a time-consuming chore that may be avoided if you pay a flat rate for material received.

AMOUNT OF COMPENSATION. Here are some hourly rates to guide you in hiring editorial and other services. Prices vary from region to region and are for 1998. These are commercial rates, fees charged by those who have overhead. Some moonlighters and freelancers may work for less. These figures are not firm and are presented here mainly for comparison.

SERVICE	HOURLY RATE
Research Discovering facts and material to be used by the author.	$20–$40
Ghosting Contract writing. You may pay your writer on a per-book, per-page or per-hour basis. The per-page or per-book ("piecework") provides you with a better idea of total project cost. The writer should also be reimbursed for expenses.	$5,000–200,000/book
Manuscript input Straight typing, double-spaced page.	$1.25/page or $15.00/hour
Copyediting Checking for grammar, spelling, punctuation and style.	$25.00–$40.00
Peer review Having another expert review the book for technical accuracy. Many will not charge to check over a chapter.	See page 124 on peer review
Content editing Fact checking and material presentation.	$25.00–$40.00
Rewriting Cleaning up the writing while retaining the author's material, approach and style.	$25.00–$40.00
Fact checking Verifying statements, statistics and facts.	$25.00–$35.00

Proofreading $20.00–$30.00
Reading galleys or bluelines against
a manuscript word for word to check
for typos, word divisions and
layout problems.

Editorial proofreading $20.00–$30.00
Proofing for continuity of style.

Indexing $2.00–$6.00/book page
Preparing the book's index.
Cost will vary depending upon technical difficulty.

Project development $25.00–$50.00
Supervising the whole project from
idea through production.

Paste-up $6.00–$20.00/page
Graphic arts work   Price varies with complexity.

Creative design $50.00
Designing and specifying typefaces, paper,
illustrations and layout.

Cover copywriting $100.00–$600.00/cover, up
Flat fee for front and back cover sales copy

Photographs, existing $20.00/up
Black-and-white print, 5 x 7
Agency fees are $150.00 for ½ page
black and white.

Photographs, shot to order $70.00 and up,
Black-and-white print, 5 x 7   depending on quantity.

Scanning $60

Illustrations, each $200 for ¼ page b/w, $250 color.
                                       $500 for full page b/w, $750 color.

Line drawings for the interior of book. $50.00
Simple graphs and charts.
The more creative the art, the more it costs.

Cover art $800.00–$2000.00
Four color including art, type and ready for
color separations.

THE ADVANCE paid to your writer seals the deal, which is an important legal consideration. It also puts pressure on both of you to perform. The advance makes the writer feel accepted and has great psychological value; the advance does not have to be large to work as an incentive. Advances generally range all the way from $100 to $15,000 and are usually in the area of 20 to 25 percent of the total. One way to create an incentive, or at least to make the writer feel continually obligated, is to make progress payments. One-fifth may be paid on signing the contract, one-fifth when the writer submits the first draft, one-fifth when he or she completes the second draft and so on.

THE ROYALTY FORMULA, traditionally, has been for the publisher to pay the author 10 percent of the list (cover) price for each hardcover book anticipated to be sold through regular channels, such as book wholesalers, bookstores and libraries. Or graduated royalties for the hardcover edition might be 10 percent of the list price on the first 5,000 books sold, 12½ percent on the next 5,000 and 15 percent on sales over 10,000. Often softcover authors command 7 percent for the first 12,000 sold and 9 percent above that number. The royalties on textbooks are generally 15 percent of net (the cover price, less 20 percent). It is common in college text publishing for royalties to jump to 18 percent of net over a certain number sold. Today, most publishers are paying six to eight percent of the net receipts on trade softcover books; nearly half what they used to pay.

If two people write the book, they split the royalties. However, you could buy all rights from your collaborator and avoid paying the split.

SUBSIDIARY RIGHTS. Most contracts call for the author and publisher to split the subsidiary rights (films, book clubs, etc.) 50-50. Many contracts give the author 50 percent for print reproductions and 90 percent of the nonprint-adaptations. Many of the big publishers barely break even on the book itself and hope to make their money on the subsidiary rights.

Unless you have a narrow field of interest or the author has very strong feelings about a particular rights area, you will want a contract that includes all possible reprint rights. Once you have published the basic book, you will want to entertain the possibilities of translations to other languages or co-publishing in other English-speaking markets. Then there are book club adoptions, film rights, magazine excerpts, newspaper serializations and the mass-market paperback rights. Your promotion will rub off on all areas, so make the most of your efforts by taking complete control of the manuscript.

COPYRIGHT CLEARANCES or permissions are the responsibility of the writer (unless you have supplied the material) and this should be spelled out in the contract. The writer knows his or her sources better than you and should be responsible for obtaining permission for extracted material, articles, photos or drawings. This includes the right to translate foreign material.

TERM AND CONTINUITY OF THE CONTRACT. The agreement may be for a stated period, say until the completion of the manuscript, or for the copyright life of the book. It should be made binding on those who succeed both sides: the heirs and so on.

SCHEDULE. Include a work timetable and a clause allowing you to cancel the agreement if the writer fails to meet deadlines; always keep the pressure on writers to perform. Your writer must turn in work regularly, while you must edit it promptly.

Use written memos to convey deadlines. A memo avoids misunderstandings and may be used as evidence should there be a dispute later.

KEEP FINAL SAY. Whether you are dealing with an editor, co-author, researcher or ghostwriter, retain final approval as to acceptability of the product produced by your partner.

Product acceptability may be worded "in form and conte satisfactory to the author" (you). This may sound a bit harsh, as it can be very subjective but someone has to steer the ship. It is your job to maintain control of all aspects of the project. Just because your partner in this work is an expert at writing does not mean he or she knows better than you what should be in your book. You are paying the bill, and you must get what you want. You may not always be right but you are always the boss.

Publishers routinely contract for books and pay advances with the understanding that the author is obligated to turn in an "acceptable" manuscript. So do not feel uncomfortable about retaining final approval. To be fair to the writer and to your project, you will probably be better off giving progressive approval, chapter by chapter.

Final say as to acceptability must be made clear at the time of the contract negotiation because you are dealing with egos. If your partner understands you have final say, he or she is less likely to sulk when you cut or change the work. Final say must be discussed during negotiation and be part of the contract. Retaining final approval is usually less of a problem when dealing with a professional writer.

If you cannot agree on the work or changes, you have the right to remove the writer from the project, while the writer has the right to keep all progress payments received.

FURTHER CLAUSES include arbitration agreements in case of dispute, a paragraph saying the contract is being entered into on the basis of "good faith" and a statement that this is the only agreement, that neither party is bound by any other discussion during the negotiations.

WORKS FOR HIRE. So-called "works (done) for hire" under the Copyright Act belong to the employer. The hired writer has no copyright interest in the material. The writer, though, can retain the copyright or a share in it if it is so specified in the employment contract or other written agreement.

f the definition of "work for hire" is very
er copyright law, the question of who is
ı employee is not very clear. The courts'
nis subject have been contradictory. In every
:ment should be signed between employer/
ıt clearly delineates who owns what copyright
interests. ⸱ ⸱ s exercise will avoid later complications.

Collaborators who normally do not have any copyright interest in the end product include persons whose work is merely research, editing, proofing, pasting up a contribution to a collection, a translation, a supplementary work, a compilation, and persons who prepare textbook material or tests, according to the Copyright Act. But if the writer's contribution is important enough, he can bargain for a share of the copyright interest, and reduce that to a written agreement. That is an enforceable contract right.

Writers who are commissioned or hired as independent contractors to work on a book or other work, including ghostwriters, are not traditional employees or hired hands. They are more creative forces who normally have copyright interests in what they produce. Again, this can be varied totally or in part by a written agreement.

In addition to the agreement, copyright interests may be established as follows: The copyright owner may sell, release or transfer in writing all or part of his or her rights. Or, separate licensing agreements for limited use may be contracted, which should also be registered in the copyright office.

As the author of a book, you may want to buy outright, or in part, any copyright interests those persons working with you may have. Then, protect that purchase by registering yourself with the copyright office as the owner, explaining on the form how you acquired ownership of the copyright. Obtain the current form from the Copyright Office, Library of Congress, Washington, DC 20559.

4 SPACE 4: Claimant(s)

Name(s) and Address(es) of Copyright Claimant(s): Give the name(s) and address(es) of the copyright claimant(s) in this work even if the claimant is the same as the author. Copyright in a work belongs initially to the author of the work (including, in the case of a work made for hire, the employer or other person for whom the work was prepared). The copyright claimant is either the author of the work or a person or organization to whom the copyright initially belonging to the author has been transferred.

Transfer: The statute provides that, if the copyright claimant is not the author, the application for registration must contain "a brief statement of how the claimant obtained ownership of the copyright." If any copyright claimant named in space 4 is not an author named in space 2, give a brief, general statement summarizing the means by which that claimant obtained ownership of the copyright. Examples: "By written contract"; "Transfer of all rights by author"; "Assignment"; "By will." Do not attach transfer documents or other attachments or riders.

From copyright Form TX

The above suggestions reflect current law but are not intended as legal advice for your specific situation. You should consult a literary attorney to help with the written documents.

protecting my rights

DRAFT ASSIGNMENT OF COPYRIGHT

This assignment of copyright is made between (the Writer) and _____ (the Author).

Whereas, the Writer has created an original work titled _____
and is the sole proprietor of the copyright in such work, and

Whereas, the Author wishes to acquire the entire interest of the Writer in said work.

Now, therefore, in consideration of $ _____ , the receipt of which is hereby acknowledged, the Writer hereby assigns and transfers to Author, his heirs, executors, administrators, and assigns, all of Writer's right, title, and interest in the said work and the copyright thereof throughout the world, including any statutory copyright together with the right to secure renewals and extension of such statutory copyright throughout the world, for the full term of said copyright or statutory copyright and any renewal or extension thereof which is or may be granted throughout the world.

In witness whereof, Writer has executed this instrument as of the day and year set forth below.

Name: _____

Witness: _____

Date: _____

Example of Assignment of Copyright

(It would be advisable to sign this assignment before a Notary Public or witness, though this is not strictly required by law.)

CONFLICT RESOLUTION. Even with a tightly written contract, the way the project was conceptualized and the way the work proceeds may be very different. The two most common problems between collaborators involve who should be listed as the first author and how the income from the book should be split. As the project proceeds, one partner may feel that she or he is contributing more than a fair share while the other partner is to receive top billing. When conflicts surface, decide first whether discussing them is worth unsettling the partnership and slowing progress on the manuscript. Conflict can kill initiative and creativity. If you decide to broach the subject, try to settle the problems by talking them through. Then if you change some of your original plans, make the needed alterations in your contract and responsibility chart.

If the problem is more serious, you might want to bring in an outside facilitator or arbitrator. Make sure this is someone neither of you know but who is familiar with the publishing profession. You and your partner have come a long way together. It would be a shame to give up on your project now.

No matter how well you plan, conflict can arise during the writing process. It is important to settle conflicts immediately, so they do not get in the way of your mission. Talk to each other, don't just stew over the problem.

You and your partner must be fair to the project as well as to each other. You must agree not to raise partnership issues just prior to a deadline. This valuable time must be spent on the manuscript, not on arguing.

Now that you are committed to a writing partner, the next question is, can you accept the stresses of authoring?

Discussion is an exchange of knowledge; argument an exchange of ignorance. — Robert Quillen

In contracts, the big print giveth and the small print taketh away.

15

WRITING AND YOUR PERSONAL LIFE

For many people, writing a book is a stressful time. Tempers run short, relationships are strained and sleep is fitful. Some authors turn to pills or drink to help them cope with their situation. Some find their resistance to colds and other communicable diseases is lower during this time. What is so stressful about writing a book? Here are what some authors say:

> "Writing is a very solitary endeavor. It is a tedious effort that requires total concentration."

> "The permanence of the written word in a book makes you vulnerable. A bad review can not only ruin your sales but it can undermine your self-esteem."

> "You have to be able to take criticism for a creative work that you have spent months or even years completing. You know this while you are writing."

> "As you get closer to the completion of your work there is an inability to think about anything else. You become addicted to getting it done. It puts a strain on your relationships and your health."

I've given my memoirs far more thought than any of my marriages. You can't divorce a book. — Gloria Swanson

"I tend to punish myself mentally until I get it down on paper."

"Writing? Oh it's easy—just sit down at your keyboard and open up a vein."

Remember, not all stress is negative. The adrenaline rush that stress creates also helps your mind and body operate at their peak. Stress may be affecting your writing adversely if:

- You make every excuse you can to keep from sitting down at your computer.
- Any small distraction breaks your train of thought and you give up for the day.
- You are tense and irritable with those around you—family, friends and colleagues.
- You can't relax and you are not sleeping well.
- You are over-indulging in food, cigarettes, alcohol or drugs.
- You wish you had never started this project.

If you find these things happening to you, you know it is time to take a break from the project, from a few days to a few weeks. It is time for a fresh perspective.

Many first-time authors are also holding down a full-time job. They find there simply is not enough time to do everything they would like. Attention to personal needs is one of the first things to go in a busy life and eliminating this time for reflection and relaxation is truly stress inducing.

Be sure to exercise regularly and give yourself some personal time.

WRITER'S BLOCK is a common problem for most writers. Usually the frustration comes when you cannot get what is in your mind down on paper.

When you get a bad case of writer's block and thinker's cramp, admit to yourself that you do not know what you want to say and remove yourself from the project to think. This might only require taking a shower or running around the block. Or it could mean taking a vacation. Another technique is to switch to an easier part of the book. Creativity cannot be forced.

Mindy Bingham's book Choices *was nearly complete in August. The only chapter left was the last one and it needed to be very creative to bring together what had been said. Mindy was stumped because she knew what she wanted to accomplish but not how. She took off on a five-week tour of Europe and left the manuscript at home. At times, while driving through the countryside, a thought or an idea would pop into her head. When she returned, she developed the exercises and wrote the final chapter in less than two hours.*

The best solution for stress and writer's block is to follow the organization in the book. Keep your manuscript in a binder, use the "pilot system" and work on the smallest and easiest areas first.

NEGOTIATING WRITING TIME WITH FAMILY, FRIENDS, EMPLOYERS AND YOURSELF. You must sit down with your family or others who are used to claiming a large percentage of your time and discuss your project and how it will affect your relationships.

Before you begin your book, negotiate writing time and writing space. Then go over your timetable so they understand just how long this project should take. An author needs all the support he or she can get. Rumpled feelings from those in the support system will only create an emotional burden that will be counterproductive. You will have to become sensitive to the feelings of isolation from your loved ones as they view with jealousy your new "love affair"—your manuscript.

It might be helpful to share the following message with those close to you before you begin:

MESSAGE TO THE LOVED ONES OF AN AUTHOR

This writing project will cost you the time and the attention of 'your author'. Writing a book takes a tremendous amount of concentration, dedication and time. If there are times you seek attention but 'your author' seems somewhere else, he or she probably is. The creative spirit and energy required to finish a book-length manuscript are all-consuming.

But this will not last forever. The book will get done. And then you can bask and delight in the limelight along with 'your author' because everyone will realize that without your support, under-standing, and encouragement the book could never have been completed.

Have you ever wondered why most authors dedicate their books to spouses and children? You will soon find out why!

Mindy and Dan

HUSBAND/WIFE TEAM. Sometimes it makes sense to involve a spouse with the project. He or she may be an equal co-author or may serve a supporting role in editing, typing or research. Working together can be beneficial to a marriage. Rather than suffering the stress resulting from dividing time between spouse and project, you can make the project something to work on together.

Negotiate a contract with your spouse the same way you would with an outsider. Not only must your roles be clear, you must agree on the time and personal commitment the book writing will receive. At this point, the potential of your writing is unknown, but earnings could turn out to be substantial. A contract now could alleviate problems with heirs (particularly in the case of second marriages) in the event of a divorce or death.

It is advisable to work through the responsibility chart in Chapter Thirteen. Clearly separate your writing lives from your personal lives. Avoid allowing professional disagreements to spill over into your personal partnership. Just because you disagree on a word, phrase or explanation, it does not follow that you love each other less.

Dr Heather Johnston Nicholson and Dr. Ralph L. Nicholson wrote Distant Hunger: Agriculture, Food and Human Values. *Both were interested in the subject, but each had a different orientation. Heather was a humanist and taught administration of public policy, and Ralph was a scientist with a background in biochemistry and botany.*

They decided to take one summer to work on the book. The Nicholsons set limitations on the project by defining the study as the only workplace. The rest of the house was off limits to their project-related discussions.

The Nicholsons complemented each other in this work. Because the book was to be addressed to the layperson, they had to find a common language that could be understood by all. It became clear when there was too much social science jargon because Ralph couldn't understand it. They knew when they were using too many biological terms because Heather couldn't understand.

I have a sign on the door that says: DO NOT COME IN. DO NOT KNOCK. DO NOT SAY HELLO. DO NOT SAY I'M LEAVING. DO NOT SAY ANYTHING UNLESS THE HOUSE IS ON FIRE . . . also, telephone's off! — Judith Krantz

During that summer they developed a deep appreciation for each other's minds and a determination to understand each other's work. Where before they had a "low contention marriage," they now gave themselves permission to disagree as professional colleagues who were seeking truth. This changed approach brought them closer together and strengthened their marriage.

TELLING FRIENDS. It is a good idea to tell your close friends what you are doing. Do not expect them to understand the incredible time and energy commitment a book-length manuscript requires. But they will begin to notice that you do not have as much time for them now. Let them know the condition is temporary.

Do not tell everyone about your project. The more people you tell about your book, the more pressure you put on yourself to produce. Pretty soon everyone who sees you will want to know how the book is coming. While talking about your topic may give you practice in presentation as well as help in formulating your thoughts, be careful not to overdo this. Save your creative energy—you don't want to talk your subject to death.

Always remember that writing books is a competitive field. Do not give your good ideas away. Do not discuss your project with other authors, especially if you are producing a pathfinding book. The cocktail party is a good place to gather information, not to reveal it.

WRITING AND YOUR EMPLOYMENT. Most first-time authors are also employed full-time. If you have a nine-to-five job this means you will have to work your writing time around these hours. Even when you are writing on your own

---

I just think it's bad to talk about one's present work, for it spoils something at the foot of the creative act. It discharges the tension. — Norman Mailer time, there are pluses and minuses in telling your employer what you are doing. Here are just a few:

The minuses:

1. Some employers may feel threatened by your project, because if your book is successful you will no longer need conventional work and may leave the company.

2. Many employers do not like their employees to moonlight. They want all your energies. Anytime you are not in top mental form, they may imagine it is due to a late night of writing.

3. Your work may be threatening to colleagues. A successful book may increase your status in the company and fellow employees may be jealous.

4. If you are writing about things you have learned in your company, your employer may feel some ownership of the material. Or your employer may be afraid you are giving away trade secrets.

The pluses:

1. An employer could feel that your efforts are giving you new skills and information, making you a more valuable employee.

2. A book establishes you as an expert and brings prestige to your company.

3. Your book will allow you to fulfill a dream and therefore make you a more contented person.

Weigh the pluses and minuses along with the temperament and policies of your employer before you reveal your new project. You may want some understanding and support during the months ahead and you may wish to ask for a short leave when you get down to the final draft.

If you have two jobs and you're rich, you have diversified interests. If you have two jobs and you're poor, you're moonlighting.

WRITING RETREATS. A you get close to the final draft of your book you will probably be less tolerant of distractions. After all, you are trying to keep an entire manuscript in your mind. This is a good time to take a quiet vacation. Or consider a sabbatical or a leave without pay to complete your work. For many people, getting away from all distraction is probably the most efficient thing to do at this stage of the project. There are writers' colonies and retreat houses. You can even check into a motel or resort to avoid distractions. Or just find a quiet room in your home, put up the 'do not disturb' sign, and unplug the phone. For the final phase, a retreat can make the difference between a good book and a great book.

AUTOGRAPHING BOOKS is something you will be asked to do both in person and by mail. It is surprising how many prolific authors have never given much thought to how they might autograph a book. Confronted with an admiring fan, they are suddenly at a loss for words. Most authors simply sign: "To Wendy with best wishes," adding their signature and sometimes the date. Try to be more personal. If there is something special about the buyer, include it in your autograph. Sometimes time does not permit more than a quick signature. But on a mail order book, you can dream up something special. And by the way, especially when rushed, make sure you spell your fan's name correctly. In all the hustle, it is easy to draw a blank and misspell the simplest name or word, ruining a book.

YOUR NEW STATUS. Your status will change from that of a private person, the "writer," to a public person, the "expert." You will have opportunities you never thought available until now. Your friends will treat you differently. Some will be

---

A celebrity is a person who works hard all his life to become known, then wears dark glasses to avoid being recognized.
— Fred Allen

happy for you and some will be jealous—jealous because they did not write the book. People new in your field will treat you like a god while those who have been around for years may be rather unkind.

Gary Glenn is a fire investigator. With his wife, Peggy, he wrote a fire safety guide titled Don't Get Burned. *The new fire fighters treated Gary with awe, while some of the old-timers felt threatened or were jealous.*

Many new authors who write a book that gets a great deal of national notice do not foresee their new popularity, their celebrity status.

Bob Johnson co-authored the first book on the tri-athlon and was instantly propelled to celebrity status. While training for the "Iron Man" competition in Hawaii, he was pursued by groupies wherever he went.

Once you become a published author, your life will change. While the whole process might be exciting and stimulating, being in the limelight may not be as much fun as you used to dream.

In the meantime, let the chart on the following page suggest some solutions to the most common hazards of being an author.

A writer's life should be a tranquil life. Read a lot and go to the movies. — Mario Puzo

THE HAZARDS OF BEING A SUCCESSFUL AUTHOR

HAZARDS	SOLUTIONS
Too much recognition	Use a pseudonym
Too many contacts	Get an unlisted phone
Jealous friends	Meet new people
Lost personal time	Say 'no' Hire help Quit your other job
Your book becomes your identity	Write a new book
Post publishing blues	Take a vacation Write a new book
Addiction to writing	Don't worry about it Write a new book

There will be other challenges. But most authors agree that the rewards of being published far outweigh the stresses. And if you can think of a job that doesn't come equipped with its own kind of challenges, let us know.

Failure is very difficult for a writer to bear, but very few can manage the shock of early success. — Maurice Valency

---

16

YOUR PUBLISHING OPTIONS

Once your book is written, you have to decide how to get it into print. Fortunately, there are several choices. Read about your options and then see the evaluation chart at the end of the chapter.

You may approach a large New York general publisher, a smaller specialized publisher or work with an agent. If you decide to self-publish, you will go to a book printer. If you choose to go your own route, you will become one of the many "small presses." As you expand your list of titles, you may find yourself with a thriving business. With drive and desire, you could one day even become a major conventional publisher. Now let's take a look at the choices by starting with some definitions.

"PUBLISH" means to prepare and issue material for public distribution or sale, or "to place before the public." The book does not have to be beautiful, it does not even have to sell, it needs only to be issued. Saleability will depend upon the content and the packaging.

A **"PUBLISHER"** is the one who puts up the money, the one who takes the financial risk. He or she has the book printed and then distributes it, hoping to make back more money than has been invested. The publisher may be a big New York firm or a first-time author but he or she is always the investor.

A "**BOOK**" by international standards is a publication with at least 49 pages not counting the covers. The U.S. Post Office will accept publications with eight or more printed pages for "book rate" postage. Books should not be confused with pamphlets, which have less than 49 pages, or periodicals. Magazines and newspapers are examples of periodicals. They are published regularly and usually carry advertising.

THE BOOK PUBLISHING INDUSTRY in the U.S. consists of more than 53,000 firms, by R. R. Bowker's count, but there are many thousands more publishers who do not bother to apply for a listing. For example, over 130 book publishers are located in Santa Barbara, California, but the *Yellow Pages* list just 10 percent of these one- and two-person firms.

About 22 publishers are considered to be the major companies, and most of them are located in New York City. Altogether, more than 60,000 people are employed in book publishing in the U.S. Sales amount to nearly $24-billion per year for the over 1.2-million active titles listed in *Books in Print.* Even though most of the books are older books that are still in print, the volume still amounts to over 300 new books each year.

THE BIG PUBLISHING FIRMS concentrate on books that anticipate audiences in the tens of thousands. Many houses were absorbed by much larger soap and oil companies in the 1970s but were sold in the early 1980s when the companies found that book publishing was not as predictably profitable as other media. A look at the economics of big publishing will help us to better understand their problems. It has been estimated that some 350,000 book-length manuscripts are written each year but that only 110,000 go into print. Many of the larger publishers receive 15,000 to 20,000 unsolicited manuscripts each year. Reading manuscripts takes an enormous amount of editorial time, and a very high percentage of the submissions are poorly written or do not fit the publisher's line; they are a waste of editorial time. Simon and Schuster says that over the years it has published less than one percent of all the unsolicited manuscripts it has received and then with modest success.

The 12,000 bookstores do not have the shelf space to display all of the 110,000 new (original and reprint) titles published each year, so they concentrate on the books that move the best. Consequently, most publishers figure that even after selecting the best manuscripts and pouring in the promotion money, only three books of ten will sell well, four will break even and three will be losers.

Ever wonder why all the books in the store have very recent copyright dates? They are seldom more than a year old because the store turns them over so fast. Shelf space is expensive and in short supply. The books either sell or go back to the publisher. If one title doesn't move, it is replaced by another.

Most initial print runs are of 5,000 books. Then the title remains "in print" (available for sale) for maybe a year. If the book sells out quickly, it is reprinted and the publisher dumps in more promotion money. If the book does not catch on, it is pulled off the market and "remaindered" (sold off very cheaply) to make room for new titles. The publisher has a business to run; there is overhead to consider and bills must be paid.

The financial demands cause him or her to be terribly objective about the line. To many publishers, in fact, a book is just a book. If they already cover a subject, they won't be interested in a new manuscript on the same topic. They already serve that interest and do not care that yours might be better. Many big publishers are not interested in whether it is a good book; they are under financial pressure to publish only books that will sell. Therefore, they concentrate on authors with good track records or Hollywood and political personalities who can move books with their names. Only

---

All of us enjoy being the hot publisher of the moment—and in paperback that designation can change every three weeks.
— Susan Petersen, President, Ballantine Books

occasionally will they accept a well-written manuscript by an unknown and then it must be on a topic with a ready and massive audience. A published writer has a much better chance of selling than an unpublished one, regardless of the quality of the work.

Large publishers usually must sell close to 10,000 copies in hardcover to break even. They hope to make their money on subsidiary rights for the paperback edition, book clubs or movie rights. They spend several thousand dollars on promoting most titles and often more than $50,000 on a blockbuster. This makes it tough on the small publisher with less volume who must compete on the basis of sales and cannot afford large-scale promotion.

Publishers, like most business people, seem to follow the "80-20" principle. That is, they spend 80 percent of their effort on the top 20 percent of their books. The remaining 20 percent of their time goes to the bottom 80 percent of their line. Most books have to sell themselves to induce the publisher to allocate more promotion money.

The author will get a royalty of 6 to 10 percent of the net receipts, usually on a sliding scale, and the economics here are not encouraging. For example, a print run of 5,000 copies of a book selling for $20 will net maybe $50,000, and a 10 percent royalty on this is $5,000. That probably is not enough money to pay for all the time spent at your computer. The chances of selling more than 5,000 copies are highly remote because after a few months, the publisher takes the book out of print. In fact, the publisher will probably report fewer sales because some books will be returned by the bookstores unsold.

If your manuscript is a blockbuster novel with potential sales in the millions, you may need a big publisher and they certainly want you. They will take care of all the printing and

---

The best and most businesslike way to write for money—and consistent publication—is to find out what editors want and try to produce it. — Kay Haugaard distributing. But if you think you can have your royalty checks sent to you in Bimini, you may be disappointed. Once a book is produced by a publishing house, authors are often expected to take an exhausting role in promotion. Many publishing houses will not even consider a "non-promotable" author anymore. They are looking for personalities as well as writing talent.

If you have written a nonfiction book, you may be asked to furnish sales leads. Whatever your book, you may be expected to go on tour. You may wind up doing most of the promotion yourself while losing control over the program. When sales drop off, you might want to buy the book and the remaining stock back from the publisher so you can pursue the marketing yourself. At this time you may also discover to your dismay that your contract provides that you must submit your next two manuscripts to this same publisher.

The big publishing houses provide a needed service, but for many first-time authors they are unapproachable. Once in, the author does not get the best deal, and getting out may be very difficult. To begin with, the publisher may keep the manuscript for months and then reject it. If your book is accepted, it may be heavily edited, or the title may be changed. Publishers say that they have invested lots of time and money to find out what will sell, but in return for their knowledge you give up some control of your project.

Some people say that the big publishers are schizophrenic in their approach—the editorial side goes after "prestige" manuscripts, while the marketing people push for what they think they can sell.

In other words, the fact that your book will probably not be accepted by one of these top publishers should not be considered a major tragedy.

If you are still interested in pursuing established publishers, give yourself the best possible chance by going

---

Someday I hope to write a book where the royalties will pay for the copies I give away. — Clarence Darrow about the submission professionally.

There is a brighter side: there are small publishers and self-publishers who are closer to their markets. They understand what the public wants to read. See FOD/WEB Document 114: *Inside Book Writing* (See Appendix).

THE SMALL PRESSES usually specialize in certain areas such as technical books, regional books, poetry, and so on. They are often new at the trade and have yet to expand out of one or two lines of books. One definition of a small press is a publisher with no more than 12 full-time staff members, issuing fewer than 25 titles per year for receipts under $400,000. Most "small presses" are much smaller.

Para Publishing reluctantly hired employees after 16 years. Each year it ships over 100,000 copies of some 30 new and revised titles for a gross in the high-six figures.

Many small presses emerged from the anti-establishment movement of the sixties, their existence made possible by the introduction of newer, simpler, cheaper (offset) printing methods. They may be small or fairly large, but nearly all are specialized. Many people in the industry are attracted by the flexibility these publishers offer. As the firms flourish, some of these talented employees break away and start new small presses of their own. There are thousands of small presses and because of their relatively low overhead, they can produce their books much more cheaply than the big publishers can.

However, while the smaller publishers may be closer to their markets, their royalty rates are the same and many do not promote a title much harder than a big publisher does. Most authors will agree that small publishers are usually nice to deal with and provide good personal attention, but they are faced with many of the same economic problems as the rest of the industry and do not always have the resources to combat them. To find a small press, consult Dustbooks' *International Directory of Little Magazines and Small Presses* and *Literary Market Place*. Look for a publisher who specializes in your type of book. Do not take a business book to a cookbook publisher. He will not take it and would not know where to sell it if he did. You want a publisher who knows the market, one who can plug your book into his promotion/distribution system.

CO-OP PUBLISHING HOUSES have been formed in many areas. Usually three to ten people join together to share the work of editing, design, layout, typesetting, compilation and financing. Often these people contribute more labor ("sweat equity") than money to the publishing venture.

VANITY PUBLISHERS publish over 1,000 titles each year; a half-dozen firms produce about 70 percent of all the subsidized books. Many of these businesses advertise in the *Yellow Pages* under "Publishers." Vanity publishers offer regular publishing services, but the author invests the money. Under this arrangement, the author pays the full publishing cost (more than just the printing bill) and receives 40 percent of the retail price of the books sold and 80 percent of the subsidiary rights, if sold. The cost is between $20,000 and $30,000 to get into print.

The vanity publisher claims he will furnish all the regular publishing services, including promotion and distribution. But according to *Writer's Digest*, vanity publishers usually do not deliver the promotion they promise and the books rarely return one-quarter of the author's investment.

The ads reading, "To the author . . . " or "Manuscripts wanted by . . . " easily catch the eye of the author with a book-length manuscript. Vanity presses almost always accept a manuscript for publication, usually with a glowing review letter. They don't make any promises regarding sales and usually the book sells fewer than 100 copies. The vanity publisher does not have to sell any books because the author has already paid for the work. Therefore, vanity publishers are interested in manufacturing the book, not in editing, promotion, sales or distribution.

Since binding is expensive, the vanity publisher often binds a few hundred copies; the rest of the sheets remain unbound unless needed. The "advertising" promised in the contract normally turns out to be only a "tombstone" ad listing your book with many other titles in *The New York Times.* Results from this feeble promotion are rare.

The review copies sent by vanity presses to book reviewers usually go straight into the "circular file." They do not like vanity presses because they know the book has not been "accepted" by any third party. Further, they know from experience that there will be little promotional effort and that the book will not be available to readers in the stores.

Only a local bookstore might be persuaded to carry an author's vanity press book. The rest know there won't be any promotional effort expended to bring the public in.

The vanity publisher can get your book into print if this is all you want and will not cut the manuscript all to pieces but, this is not the least expensive way to go. It would make more sense to contract with a book packager to handle the whole job. Publishing yourself should save considerably over vanity publishing.

Before considering a vanity publisher, send for *Should You Pay to Have It Published?* ($1.00 from Writer's Digest, 1507 Dana Avenue, Cincinnati, OH 45207-9988.) From everything you read, it appears that no one likes vanity publishers. Some have been in trouble with the Federal Trade Commission (FTC), and one was successfully sued by a client author in 1990.

BOOK PRODUCERS are packagers who take your idea and then handle the writing, editing, illustrating, design, layout and printing. They deliver the books to you and you handle the marketing, billing and collecting. Many packagers

---

What an agent is supposed to do is ensure there is a competitive spirit when a publisher buys a book.
— Theron Raines, agent

specialize in certain areas, such as children's books, so shop around. A list of book producers can be found in *Literary Market Place.*

LITERARY AGENTS provide a valuable service to publishers by screening out the not-yet-ready manuscripts. Most new material comes to big publishers through them. Agents have to serve the publisher well, for if they submit a poor manuscript, the publisher will never give them another appointment. Therefore, agents like sure bets, too, and are reluctant even to consider an unpublished writer. When they do, their fee is often higher than their normal commission of 15 percent.

For the author, agents will make manuscript suggestions, negotiate the contract and try to sell the book to one of their many contacts; agents will exploit all possible avenues. If your manuscript is a winner, it is wise to have professional management.

According to *Literary Agents Marketplace,* about 40 percent of the book agents will not read manuscripts by unpublished authors and a good 15 percent will not even answer query letters from them. Of those agents who will read the manuscript of an unpublished author, 80 percent will charge for the service. 80 percent of the agents will not represent professional books; 93 percent will not touch reference works; 99 percent will not handle technical books; 98 percent will not represent regional books, satire, musicals and other specialized manuscripts. While most agents will handle novel-length fiction, only 20 percent are willing to take on either novelettes or short stories, and only 2 percent have a special interest in literature or quality fiction.

On the fringe, there are a number of "agents" who charge a "reading fee" and then pay students to read and critique the manuscript. They make their money on these fees, not from placing the manuscripts.

You may contact agents by mail. Send a query letter and a two to three page synopsis. The letter should describe the book and its intended market. Describe your background and request permission to send the entire manuscript. For a list of literary agents, see *Writer's Market* and *Literary Market Place*. Also write for a list to The Society of Authors' Representatives (PO. Box 650, New York, NY 10113). Agents specialize, so look for one who handles your type of book.

Must reading for anyone approaching an agent or conventional publisher is *How To Get Happily Published* by Judith Appelbaum.

... but doesn't sound like the way to go X

PUBLISHING OPTIONS

Consider the following statements to help decide which publishing option is best for you.

Conventional publisher If you feel:

1. It is important to me to be published by a major New York publisher because I value the type of recognition that would bring.
2. I have a personal connection with a publisher. I know an editor and can get my manuscript considered.
3. Publishers and their editors will change my manuscript for the better. I trust their judgment.
4. I will be happy to accept a 10 percent royalty.
5. Rejection does not bother me. I will keep sending out my manuscript until I find the right publisher.

Then start trying to find a conventional publisher.

Vanity press If you feel:
1. I want a few copies of my book for family and friends. It does not have to sell.
2. I am not concerned about price or about getting a return on my investment.
3. I do not want to produce my own book.

Then a vanity press might serve your purposes well. (A vanity press is rarely a good choice.)

Book producer or packager If you feel:
1. I want an attractive, professional-looking book.
2. I want someone else to handle the details; to take my manuscript and deliver the books to me to sell.

A book producer might be your answer.

Agent If you feel:
1. I do not have the time to find a publisher.
2. I would rather create than sell.
3. I am confident of my talent as a writer.

You should try to find an agent.

Self-publishing If you feel:
1. I am businesslike as well as creative.
2. I can afford to invest in a business.
3. I want to maintain complete control over my book.
4. If I wait much longer, someone else will beat me to the market.
5. I want a business of my own and I am willing to put in the time and effort necessary.
6. I want to maximize the return on my efforts.

Self-publishing might be the route for you.

Which option matches your skills and meets your needs? If you select self-publishing, you will be especially interested in the next chapter.

When one door closes, another opens, but we often look so long and regretfully upon the closed door, we do not see the ones which open for us. — Alexander Graham Bell

17

SELF-PUBLISHING

IN SELF-PUBLISHING the author bypasses all the middlemen, deals directly with the printer and then handles the marketing and distribution. He or she maintains complete control over the product. The self-publisher invests time as well as money, but the rewards are greater. The self-publisher gets it all.

Self-publishing is not new. It is almost a tradition. Many authors have elected to go their own way after being turned down by regular publishers. Others have decided to go their own way from the beginning. Well-known self-publishers include Mark Twain, Zane Grey, Upton Sinclair, Carl Sandburg, James Joyce, D.H. Lawrence, Ezra Pound, Edgar Rice Burroughs, Stephen Crane, Mary Baker Eddy, George Bernard Shaw, Edgar Allen Poe, Rudyard Kipling, Henry David Thoreau, Walt Whitman, Robert Ringer, Richard Nixon and many, many more.

IS YOUR BOOK A GOOD CANDIDATE FOR SELF-PUBLISHING? Some topics are especially likely to be successful in a self-published format. Your book might be if it is:

- Of interest to a specific group of people that you know how to reach.
- Likely to take a while to catch on with the public because it deals with a topic that is new or different.

- Of local or regional interest.
- Full of information needed by a certain group of people (cat owners, rose gardeners, do-it-yourselfers).
- Written specifically for your colleagues or your students.
- A philosophical or political treatise.

Since 1969, Dan Poynter has sold well over a million copies of his books, while Mindy Bingham's first book netted $112,000 in its first year. Today Mindy's company, Academic Innovations, founded in 1990, has sales of over $1.5 million with her 5 self-published titles. Naturally, they are strong advocates of self-publishing.

There are thousands of small author-publisher firms, many of them in California. Small press publishing is not "poverty publishing." Some are growing and some are withering, but practically all are hanging on. They are proving that a self-published book is not inferior to one marketed by a big New York firm. Some self-publishers are very successful and some are making a lot of money.

Self-publishing is not difficult. In fact, it may even be easier than dealing with a publisher. The job of the publishing manager is not to perform every task, but to see that every task gets done. The self-publisher deals directly with the printer and handles as many of the editing, proofing, promotion and distribution tasks as he or she can. What he can't do, he farms out. Therefore, self-publishing may take on many forms depending on the author's interests, assets and abilities. It allows you to concentrate on those creative and business areas you find most challenging and fun.

Properly planned, there is little monetary risk in self-publishing. If you follow the plan, the only variable is the subject of the book. Poetry and fiction are difficult to sell, but

---

The cost of publishing a book is no more than the cost of a year in a good college and publishing a book is a year in a good college.

most nonfiction topics sell and can be profitable. In fact, many authors publish themselves because this method provides the best return on their labor. The big publisher only gives the book a short time to flourish or fail. The self-publisher, on the other hand, uses the first year to build a solid market for a future of sustained sales. While a big publisher may sell only 5,000 copies total, the self-publisher can often count on sales of 5,000 or more each year, year after year. Here are eight good reasons to self-publish:

1. **To make more money.** Why accept six percent to ten percent in royalties when you can have as much as 35 percent? You know your subject and you know the people in the field. You may know better than some distant publisher where to find the buyers. While the trade publisher may have some good contacts, he may not know the market as well as you, and you are undoubtedly more committed to the book. Ask yourself this question: will the trade publisher be able to sell four times as many books as I can?

   The return for time invested becomes even more important when producing a highly technical work which has a small audience.

2. **Speed.** Most publishers work on a one-and-a-half-year production cycle. Can you wait that long to get into print? Will you miss your market? The 1½ years begins after the sale of the manuscript and the conclusion of the contract negotiations. Publication could be three years away! Why waste valuable time shipping your manuscript around to see if there is a publisher out there who likes it? Richard Nixon self-published *Real Peace* in 1983 because he felt his message was urgent; he could not wait for a publisher's machinery to grind out the book.

The oldest books are still only just out to those who have not read them. — Samuel Butler

Typically, bookstores buy the first book to come out on a popular subject. Books published later may be better, but the buyer might pass on them since the store already has the subject "covered." If your book is on a subject popular right now, you might want to self-publish.

3. **To keep control of your book.** According to *Writer's Digest*, 60 percent of the big publishers do not give the author final approval on copyediting. Twenty-three percent never give the author the right to select the title, 20 percent do not consult the author on the jacket design and 36 percent rarely involve the author in the book's promotion.

   The big New York trade publishers may have more promotional connections than you, but with a whole stable of books to push, your book may get lost in the shuffle. If you self-publish, at least you can be sure that your book is in the hands of someone who cares—you.

4. **Save your energy.** Unless you are a movie star, noted politician or have a recognizable name, as a first time author it is nearly impossible to attract a big publisher.

5. **Self-publishing is good business.** There are far more tax advantages for an author-publisher than there are for an author.

6. **Self-publishing will teach you to think like a publisher.** You will learn the industry and will have a better understanding of the big picture. This can't help but make your manuscript stronger.

   A book is a product of one's self. An analogy may be drawn with giving birth. The author naturally feels that his book is terrific and that it would sell better if only his publisher would promote it more. He is very protective about his book (ever try to tell a mother her child is

---

Every imaginative production must contain some element of risk.— Paul Horgan ugly?). The publisher answers that he is not anxious to dump more money into a book that is not selling. So, if the author self-publishes, he or she gains a better understanding of the arguments on both sides. It is his or her money and choice.

7. **You will gain self-confidence.** You will be proud to be the author of a printed book. Compare this feeling with pleading with people to read your manuscript.

8. **Finally, you may have no other choice.** There are more manuscripts than can be read. Most publishers will not even look at your manuscript. Just because your manuscript has not been read by a publisher does not mean it isn't worth publishing. Even a rejection slip after a reading is no sign of poor quality—your book may not fit their product line. If you know your field and are receiving positive feedback from your peers, you should go ahead and publish the book yourself.

SHOULD YOU SELF-PUBLISH? Would-be author-publishers should be cautioned that self-publishing is not for everyone. Writing is an art while publishing is a business, and many people are unable to do both well.

In self-publishing, once the manuscript has been completed, the creative spirit must give way to the entrepreneur and the promoter. For some people, this is simply too schizophrenic. But for those who can make the transition, self-publishing is arguably the most satisfying and lucrative way to get into print.

Take the following quiz to help determine if you are a good candidate for self-publishing.

An entrepreneur spends 16 hours a day to avoid having to work for someone else for eight hours. — James Healey

SELF-PUBLISHING EVALUATION

Check the box that best describes you or your feelings.

Entrepreneurial spirit

☒ 1. I like being in control. I like to have the final say on the direction of my projects.

☐ 2. I like to have someone else make the final decisions after I give my input.

☐ 3. I would rather be given direction and do not want too much responsibility.

Ability to risk capital

☐ 1. I have money I can afford to risk in my business ventures.

☐ 2. I'm willing to invest my time but not my money in my writing projects.

☒ 3. I want assured compensation for my writing.

Ability to 'toot your own horn'

☒ 1. I have something to share with others and I need to make sure they know about it.

☐ 2. While I am a modest person, I know that books need promotion to sell so I will do it.

☐ 3. I would have a hard time promoting my own work. It would seem like boasting.

Independence

☐ 1. Most of all I want to be my own boss.

☒ 2. While I consider myself independent, I don't want to make all the decisions about the book by myself.

☐ 3. Being on my own really scares me. I would rather have the security of being an employee and let someone else worry about the problems.

Time to promote your book

☒ 1. I realize that writing a book is only the tip of the iceberg. I am ready for the time demands of promotion.

☐ 2. I'll spend time on promotion but I don't want the major responsibility or time demands.

☐ 3. All I want to do is finish the manuscript. I do not want to spend any more time on this project. I want to go on to something else.

Business acumen

☐ 1. I consider myself realistic and "street wise" when it comes to business.

☒ 2. Most business situations make sense, but there are areas where I need experience.

☐ 3. I am inexperienced or impractical in business matters.

Public image

☐ 1. I love to speak in front of audiences and feel I have something important to say.

☒ 2. I need some confidence in public speaking and presence but I am willing to learn.

☐ 3. I'm a private person. I do not want to make public presentations or be recognized in a crowd.

Goal oriented

☒ 1. Once I know what I want, I cannot be distracted from my goal.

☒ 2. I need someone to help me stay on track. Otherwise I take more detours than I should.

☐ 3. I have a hard time deciding what it is I really want.

Promotion and publicity

☑ 1. If I believe in a product, I have the enthusiasm and the people-skills to sell it.

☐ 2. I don't like front line sales but I can promote something if an agent opens the door for me.

☐ 3. I don't feel comfortable with sales and promotion at all. It is not dignified.

Now score yourself. Record below how many number one answers you checked, how many number two answers and how many number three answers.

_5_ Quantity of number one boxes checked

_3_ Quantity of number two boxes checked

_1_ Quantity of number three boxes checked

Review your answers. If you checked mostly number ones you would be happiest and most satisfied self-publishing. If you checked a majority of number twos, a traditional publishing route is probably best for you. If you checked a lot of number threes, you should reconsider authoring a book. If you want your book accepted beyond your immediate circle of family and acquaintances, it may be a very frustrating or negative experience for you.

This evaluation was written to identify your potential in producing a financially successful book. If your book is meant to be a family heirloom, just something you want to do for yourself, or a monument to your area of life study, you probably have no alternative to self-publishing.

Generally speaking, a large New York publisher may be more successful selling fiction while you may make more money publishing your own nonfiction. You must decide whether you wish to write, publish and/or make money.

It is possible to self-publish fiction, or at least some people are doing it, but it isn't easy. Dorothy Bryant, a novelist in Berkeley, California, successfully publishes and promotes what she writes. She calls her publishing company Ata Books.

Fiction can also make money when published on a smaller scale according to a proven formula.

John Martin at Black Sparrow Press in Santa Rosa, California, publishes only good fiction and poetry— defined as that fiction and poetry he likes. He has published many well-known authors and knows what he is doing, blending creative work with business. With years of experience, he can predict how his books will sell and has many standing orders. Each book is produced in a precise number of softcover, hardcover and signed editions. His success in selling fiction and poetry is well known.

You can take the author's royalty and the publisher's profit, all of the reward, by being both of them. Now, in addition to achieving the wealth and prestige of a published author, you can propel yourself into your own lucrative business: a publishing house. This shortcut not only makes more money (why share it?) but also saves you the time and trouble required to sell your manuscript to a publisher.

MAIL ORDER. Today, more books are sold through the mail than through bookstores. In fact, books are the leading mail order product. One-third of all these books are in the "how to" category. Mail order is considered one of the best ways for the beginner to start a venture of his or her own. Selling books by mail is a good, solid day-to-day business opportunity.

Mail order is not only the simplest way to distribute books, it is an ideal way to build a second income or a new life. You do not have to give up your job, there is little overhead, there are tax breaks, you work for yourself and the business can be operated anywhere: you need only be near a post office. No one knows about your age, education, race or sex; your opportunities are indeed equal.

Mail order marketing is like fishing. You throw out a line by promoting your products and you find out almost immediately if you have made a sale. Every day is like Christmas; opening envelopes and finding checks is great fun.

Initially, you will store your books in a closet and will slip them into padded bags for mailing. It is really quite easy and starting out is not expensive or time consuming.

Your writing/publishing/mail order company is actually combining three profitable fields and concentrating on only the best parts of each. A business of your own is the great American dream and it is still attainable. In your own business, you make the decisions to meet only those challenges you find interesting. This is not "goofing off," it is making more effective use of your time; "working smarter, not harder." You only have so much time, so make the most of it.

Running your own enterprise will provide you with many satisfying advantages. You should earn more money because you are working for yourself rather than sharing your efforts with someone else. You have job security and never have to worry about a surprise pink slip. If your writing is something you do in your spare time, you always have your regular job to fall back on. You start at the top, not the bottom, in your own company, and you work at your own pace and schedule. You will meet interesting people because as an author and publishing executive, they will seek you out.

In your own small business, if you decide to make it a full-time job, you may work when and where you wish; you do not have to go where the job is. You can work 'til dawn, sleep 'til

---

Whenever you see a successful business, someone once made a courageous decision. — Peter Drucker noon, rush off to Hawaii without asking permission: this is flexibility not available to the clock punchers.

A NOTE TO ACADEMICS. "Publish or perish" is a phrase familiar to all academics who wish to be promoted within the university system. At many schools, whether or not you have published articles or better yet, books, is an important consideration in determining tenure.

When queried about self-publishing, an eminent professor in a highly technical field who sat on the peer review committee for a major university responded quickly that self-published works are given little credence at review time. This is probably true in most schools. In further discussion with this professor about what a self-published work 'really is' and the advantages it has for the dissemination of important information, he began to look at the option in a different light. The discussion ended with him considering self-publishing the book he really wanted to write which had a much narrower audience than his publisher wanted to pursue.

Academic review committees must learn to judge books strictly on the written review the work receives by peers and in appropriate journals. Commercial publishers are in the business of making money. They make decisions on what is 'worthy' of publishing based on the size of the audience or, in other words, how many books they are going to sell.

If you are an academician who must "publish or perish," if you have a book inside you that will add to world knowledge and if you feel that your book will not be what you envisioned if you are forced to work with a commercial publisher, you should seriously consider self-publishing. But first be sure to educate your academic review committee about the advantages and credibility of self-publishing.

It is impossible for ideas to compete in the marketplace if no forum for their presentation is provided or available.
— Thomas Mann

SELF-PUBLISHING AND CHARITABLE ORGANIZATIONS.
As funding for many charitable organizations is cut back, agencies are faced with a greater need to become self-sufficient. And publishing a book can be a terrific fund-raiser. Every organization has staff members or volunteers with expertise or information the public is willing to pay for. Junior League cookbooks have supported many programs around the country. If your favorite charity is having financial challenges, you might consider helping it out by organizing, writing and publishing a book for it to sell. It beats having a bake sale!

Self-published, Choices *netted $250,000 for the Girls Club of Santa Barbara in its first two years. The added income meant that the Girls Club could continue offering low cost childcare to needy families.*

SELLING OUT. Many self-publishers find that once their books become proven moneymakers, the big publishers come to them with offers to print a new edition. Some authors use self-publishing to break into the big time. Others keep on self-publishing, keeping the work and the money to themselves.

Being an author-publisher sounds like a good life and it does make good business sense. Working for yourself requires organization and discipline but work doesn't seem so hard when you are counting your own money. To find out more about do-it-yourself book publishing, see *The Self-Publishing Manual* by Dan Poynter.

Well, what is the verdict? Are you ready to take the plunge? Is it time to get that "book inside you" out? All you have to do to start the process is make the decision and develop your plan.

If you decide to begin, we hope the "book inside you" will emerge like a butterfly from a cocoon—luminous, vibrant and ready to fly.

PERSONAL DECLARATION

On this date, _June 6, 2010_ , I, _Jan Cooper_ ,
am beginning my book with the working title of
Lay Dawn Beside me .

My primary motive(s) for authoring this book is/are
Creative Expression - making a Connection.

The audience for this book is _18 +_
My projected timetable is: _on the Best Sellers List By Jan 1, 2011_
    To complete the initial research by _DONE_
    To complete the first draft by _June 15, 2010_
    To complete the second draft(s) by _July 15, "_
    To complete the third draft by _Aug. 1, "_
    To complete the final draft by _Aug .15, "_

I have shared and discussed these plans with my family
and/or loved ones and they sign below to acknowledge
their support of this project.

signature: _____
signature: _____
signature: _____
signature: _____

I will/will not need to collaborate with partners.

    If I will, I need to locate: (circle the appropriate)
    Co-author(s)   Content editor
    Writing partner   Copyeditor
    Ghostwriter   Typist/word processor
    Contract writer   Other: _____

I am going to pursue the following publishing option(s):
(circle appropriate)
   ~~Conventional publisher~~
   Small publisher
   Vanity press
   Book producer (packager)
   Agent
   ~~Self-publishing~~

I have to get the following resource books for further study:

Title   *Author(s)*

_____   *nicholas Sparks*

_____

_____

_____

_____

_____

_____

_____

_____

I am fully aware that the authoring of a book takes a tremendous amount of time and hard work. I have the desire and the perseverance to complete this project. I am ready to accept the challenge.

   signature _____

Always bear in mind that your own resolution to succeed is more important than any other one thing.
— Abraham Lincoln

AFTERWORD

"We learn by doing," and your first book will be your most difficult. "We learn by our mistakes," and, hopefully, through the use of this book your mistakes will be small ones. We hope it introduces and guides you to a richer, more rewarding life. We also learn from others and profit from their experience by not re-inventing the wheel. There are several books every author should read and keep in his or her library. Start with these three: *How to Get Happily Published* by Judith Appelbaum, *Write Right!* by Jan Venolia and *The Self-Publishing Manual* by Dan Poynter. These books may be found at your public library, better bookstores or by ordering from Para Publishing. See the order blank on the last page.

Send to Para Publishing for a free *Publishing Information Kit.*

Write: P O Box 8206-P, Santa Barbara, CA 93118-8206; call (800) PARAPUB or email info@ParaPublishing.com.

The first step, the next one, is up to you. We hope you take it. As you write, refer to this manual. As you learn the business, make notes in it. Let us know where this book may be improved. Tell us your experiences (you may find your story in future editions). When you do get that first book into print, please send us a copy—autographed, of course.

Mindy Bingham
Dan Poynter

No horse has ever won a race it didn't enter.

If we encounter a man of rare intellect, we should ask him what books he read. — Ralph Waldo Emerson

APPENDIX
Resources

Now you can find even more specific information on writing and publishing. If, for example, you are writing and or publishing a cookbook, get all the books on how to write, produce, publish and sell cookbooks. To avoid re-inventing the wheel: learn from the experience of others. To be successful, you must have the best tools and the best resources. We have placed the specialized writing and publishing books into groups. Explanations, where they occur, are brief since it is assumed you will collect all the how-to's in your area of interest. Most books have resource sections and ideas that will lead you to more information. Do not be overly concerned with page counts v. price. Some shorter books are in larger format and some are in hard cover.

The least-expensive place to find dictionaries, style manuals and other reference books is in used bookstores. Some of the books listed may be out of print. Search for them through a used bookstore or an online bookstore.

HOW TO ORDER BOOKS. Add $4.00 for air shipping and applicable sales tax when ordering from publishers in your state. Books from larger publishers will arrive much sooner if ordered through your local bookstore or an on-line service such as Amazon.com. Some books are available from Para Publishing and are marked in parenthesis. Order from Para Publishing, PO Box 8206-146, Santa Barbara, CA 93118-8206, call (800) PARAPUB or email orders@ParaPublishing.com.

Ordering addresses of some publishers are given. Writer's Digest is mentioned many times. To save space, their address is given just once, here: **Writer's Digest Books**, 1507-P Dana Avenue, Cincinnati, OH 45207. Place credit card orders toll free: (800) 289-0963. Please mention Para Publishing when you call.

FICTION

The Complete Guide to Writing Fiction by Barnaby Conrad and the Staff of the Santa Barbara Writers' Conference. A 31-chapter anthology. $17.95. Writer's Digest Books.

How to Write and Sell Historical Fiction by Persia Woolley. $17.99. Writer's Digest Books.

Handbook of Short Story Writing, Vol. I by Frank Dickson & Sandra Smythe. $9.95. Writer's Digest Books.

Handbook of Short Story Writing, Vol. II by Jean, M. Fredette. $12.99. Writer's Digest Books.

Writing the Short Story: A Hands-On Program by Jack M. Bickham. $16.99. Writer's Digest Books.

Story Writing by Edith Ronald Mirrielees. $8.95. The Writer, 120 Boylston Street, Boston, MA 02116. Tel: (617) 423-3157 or (888) 273-8214, Fax: (617) 423-2168 E-mail: writer@user1.channel1.com Web: www.channel1.com/thewriter/

Guide to Fiction Writing by Phyllis A. Whitney. $14.20 ppd. The Writer, 120 Boylston Street, Boston, MA 02116. Tel: (617) 423-3157 or (888) 273-8214 Fax: (617) 423-2168 E-mail: writer@user1.channel1.com Web: www.channel1.com/thewriter/

Writing the Blockbuster Novel by Albert Zuckerman. $17.99. Writer's Digest Books.

How to Write a Damn Good Novel by James Frey. $15.00. St Martins Press.

How to Write a Damn Good Novel, II: Advanced Techniques for Dramatic Storytelling by James Frey. $17.95. St Martins Press.

How to Write & Sell Your First Novel by Oscar Collier and Frances Spatz Leighton. $16.99. Writer's Digest Books.

Creating Short Fiction by Damon Knight. $13.95. St. Martin's Press.

The Writer's Digest Handbook to Novel Writing by Editors of Writer's Digest. $14.99. Writer's Digest Books.

Turning Life into Fiction by Robin Hemley. $14.99. Writer's Digest Books.

Building Fiction: How to Develop Plot & Structure by Jesse Lee Kercheval. $16.99. Story Press.

Stein on Writing: A Master Editor of Some of the Most Successful Writers of Our Century Shares His Craft Techniques and Strategies by Sol Stein. $23.95. St. Martin's Press.

Learning How to Write Fiction From the Masters by Barnaby Conrad. $12.95. Plume.

How to Write Short Stories by Sharon Sorenson. $9.95. MacMillian General Reference.

POETRY

How to Publish Your Poetry: The First-Ever Marketing Manual and Success Guide for Poets by Thomas A. Williams, Ph.D. $19.95. Venture Press, Tom Williams, 12445 NW, Coral Springs, FL 33071 Tel: (800) 360-4511 E-mail: publish@gate.net Web: www.pubmart.com

The Poet's Guide to Getting Published. Free report. The National Library of Poetry, 1 Poetry Plaza, Owings Mills, MD 21117. Tel: (410) 356-2000 or (800) 694-7320 Fax: (410) 356-9931 Web: www.poetry.com or www.poets.com

Writing Poetry: Where Poems Come From and How-To Write Them by David Kirby. $12.20 postpaid. The Writer, 120 Boylston Street, Boston, MA 02116. Tel: (617) 423-3157 or (888) 273-8214 Fax: (617) 423-2168 E-mail: writer@user1.channel1.com Web: www.channel1.com/thewriter/

Poet's Market: 1800 Places to Publish Your Poetry (Annual) edited by Chantelle Bentley & Tara A. Horton. $22.99. Writer's Digest Books.

Poet's Handbook by Judson Jerome. $10.95. Writer's Digest Books.

Creating Poetry by John Drury. $18.99. Writer's Digest Books.

The Art & Craft of Poetry by Michael J. Bugeja. $19.99. Writer's Digest Books.

How to Write Poetry by Nancy Bogen. $8.00. Prentice Hall. Imprint of Simon & Shuster. 1 Lake Street, Upper River, NJ 07458. Tel: (201) 236-7000 Web: www.prenhall.com

The Poet's Companion: A Guide to the Pleasures of Writing Poetry by Kim Addonizio and Dorianne Laux. $13.00. W.W. Norton & Company.

Poemcrazy by Susan Goldsmith Wooldrige. $13.00. Crown Publications.

Poem-Making: Ways to Begin Writing Poetry by Myra Cohn Livingston. $16.95. HarperCollins Juvenile Books.

In the Palm of Your Hand: A Poet's Portable Workshop: A Lively and Illuminating Guide for the Practicing Poet by Steve Kowit and Dorianne Laux. $14.95. Tibury House Publications.

How to Write, Recite, and Delight in Your Own Poetry by Joy N. Hulme and Donna W. Guthrie. $24.90. Millbrook Press, 2 Old New Milford Road, Brookfield, CT 06804. Web: www.neca.com/mall/millbrook

Poet's Handbook by Lincoln B. Young. $11.95. Fine Arts Press, P.O. Box 3491, Knoxville, TN 37927. Tel: (423) 637-9243.

HORROR, SCIENCE FICTION AND FANTASY

How to Write Science Fiction and Fantasy by Orson Scott Card. $14.99. Writer's Digest Books.

How to Write Tales of Horror, Fantasy & Science Fiction edited by J.N. Williamson. A 27-chapter anthology. Resources. $14.99. Writer's Digest Books.

The Craft of Writing Science Fiction That Sells by Ben Bova. $16.95. Writer's Digest Books.

Science Fiction and Fantasy Writer's Sourcebook edited by David H. Borcherding. $19.99. Writer's Digest Books.

How to Write Science Fiction by Matthew Costello. $9.95. Shooting Star Press.

Dark Thoughts on Writing: Advice and Commentary from Fifty Masters of Fear and Suspense edited by Stan Wiater. $13.00. Underwood Books.

The Craft of Writing Science Fiction that Sells by Ben Bova. $16.99. Writer's Digest Books.

Aliens and Alien Societies (Science Fiction Writing Series) by Stan Schmidt and Ben Bova. $17.99. Writer's Digest Books.

Writing Horror edited by Mort Castle and Stanley Wiater. $17.99. Writer's Digest Books.

How to Write Tales of Horror, Fantasy and Science Fiction edited by J.N. Williamson. $14.99. Writer's Digest Books.

Paragons: Twelve Master Science Fiction Writers Ply Their Craft edited by Robin Scott Wilson. $14.95. St. Martin's Press.

Space Travel (Science Fiction Writing Series) by Ben Bova and Anthony R. Lewis. $16.99. Writer's Digest Books.

Time Travel (Science Fiction Writing Series) by Paul J. Nahin. $16.99. Writer's Digest Books.

World-Building (Science Fiction Writing Series) by Stephen L. Gillett and Ben Bova. $16.99. Writer's Digest Books.

ROMANCES

How to Write Romances by Phyllis Taylor Pianka. Complete how-to with resources. $15.99. Writer's Digest Books.

How to Write Erotica by Valerie Kelly. $12.00. Random House, 1992.

How to Write a Romance & Get It Published by Kathryn Falk. $5.99. New American Library. 375 Hudson Street, New York, NY 10014. Tel: (212) 366-2000.

Writing Romances: A Handbook by the Romance Writers of America edited by Rita Gallagher and Rita Clay Estrada. $18.99. Writers Digest Books.

Romance Writer's Sourcebook: Where to Sell Your Manuscripts edited by David H. Borcherding. $19.99. Writers Digest Books.

Writing Romance by Vanessa Grant. $15.95. Self Counsel Press.

MYSTERIES

How to Write Mysteries by Shannon O'Cork. Writing and marketing. $14.99. Writer's Digest Books.

Writing the Modern Mystery by Barbara Norville. From writing through launching your manuscript. $14.99. Writer's Digest Books.

How to Write and Sell Mystery Fiction by Sylvia K. Burack. Resources. $12.00. The Writer, 120 Boylston Street, Boston, MA 02116. Tel: (617) 423-3157 or (888) 273-8214 Fax: (617) 423-2168 E-mail: writer@user1.channel1.com Web: www.channel1.com/thewriter/

Writing Mysteries: A Handbook by the Mystery Writers of America by Sue Grafton. $18.99. Writer's Digest Books.

How to Write a Mystery by Larry Beinhart. $11.00. Ballantine Books.

Modus Operandi: A Writer's Guide to How Criminals Work by Mauro V. Corvasce and Joseph R. Paglino. $16.99. Betterway Publications.

Mystery Writer's Sourcebook: Where to Sell Your Manuscripts edited by David H. Borcherding and Don Prues. $19.99. Writers Digest Books.

Writing Crime and Suspense Fiction and Getting Published by Lesley Grant-Adamson. $10.95. Teach Yourself Series.

Writing the Private Eye Novel: A Handbook by the Private Eye Writers of America edited by Robert J. Randisi. $18.99. Writers Digest Books.

The Writer's Complete Crime Reference Book by Martin Roth. $19.99. Writer's Digest Books.

CHILDREN'S BOOKS

The Making of a Picture Book by Rodney Martin and John Snow. Gareth Stevens Children's Books, 1555 North River Center Drive, #201, Milwaukee, WI 53212. Tel: (414) 225-0333 or (800) 542-2595 Fax: (414) 225-0377 Web: www.gsinc.com

How to Write and Sell Children's Picture Books by Jean E. Karl. $16.95. Writers Digest Books.

Children's Writer's Word Book by Alijandra Mogilner. $19.95. Writers Digest Books.

How to Write and Illustrate Children's Books and Get Them Published edited by Treld Pelkey Bicknell and Felicity Trotman. An anthology in color. $22.50. Writer's Digest Books.

Writing Books for Young People by James Gross Giblin. Fiction and nonfiction for the five age groups. $12.00. The Writer, 120 Boylston Street, Boston, MA 02116. Tel: (617) 423-3157 or (888) 273-8214 Fax: (617) 423-2168 E-mail: writer@user1.channel1.com Web: www.channel1.com/thewriter/

Writing For Children & Teenagers by Lee Wyndham & Arnold Madison. Writing formula for fiction and nonfiction. A revised classic. Marketing and resources. $12.95. Writer's Digest Books.

How to Write, Illustrate and Design Children's Books by Frieda Gates. $23.50. Library Research Associates.

Children's Writers & Illustrator's Market: 850 Places to Sell your Work (Serial) edited by Alice P. Buening. $19.99. Writer's Digest Books.

Writing and Illustrating Children's Books for Publication: Two Perspectives by Berthe Amos and Eric Suben. $24.95. Writers Digest Books.

How to Write a Children's Book and Get it Published by Barbara Seuling. $14.00. Macmillan.

Dreams and Wishes: Essays on Writing for Children by Susan Cooper. $18.00. Published by Margaret McElderry.

NONFICTION BOOKS

Write & Grow Rich, Using Speech Recognition to Dictate Your How-to Book by Dan Poynter. $14.95 Para Publishing.

Is There a Book Inside You? Writing Alone or with a Collaborator by Dan Poynter and Mindy Bingham. $14.95. Para Publishing. Also available in a six-cassette audio album. Also see http://www.ParaPublishing.com

How to Write & Sell Your First Nonfiction Book by Oscar Collier and Frances Leighton. $9.95. St. Martins Press.

How to write a Book in 53 Days: The Elements of Speed Writing Necessity and Benefits Too by Don Paul. $14.95. Path Finder Publications.

Writing Your Book by Dan Poynter. This videotape produced by Para Publishing is an easy-to-use writing recipe for professionals who are ready to achieve celebrity status. $29.95. Available from Para Publishing.

SCIENTIFIC/TECHNICAL/MEDICAL

How to Write and Publish a Scientific Paper by Robert A. Day. $16.95. Oryx Press, 4041 N. Central Ave., Suite #700, Phoenix, AZ 85012. Tel: (602) 265-2651 Fax: (602) 265-6250 E-mail: info@oryxpress.com Web: www.oryxpress.com

Essentials for the Scientific and Technical Writer by Hardy Hoover. $7.95. Dover Publications, 31 East Second Street, Mineola, NY 11501.

Successful Scientific Writing: A Step-By-Step Guide for Biomedical Scientists by Janice R. Matthews, John M. Bowen and Robert W. Matthews. $19.95. Cambridge University Press.

A Field Guide for Science Writers: The Official Guide of the National Association of Science Writers edited by Deborah Blum and Mary Knudson. $25.00. Oxford University Press.

Scientific Style and Format: The CBE Manual for Authors, Editors and Publishers by Edward J. Huth. $39.95. Cambridge University Press.

Scientific English: A Guide for Scientists and Other Professionals by Robert A. Day. $19.00. Oryx Press.

Science As Writing by David Millard Locke. $35.00. Yale University Press.

How to Write and Publish Engineering Papers and Reports by Herbert B. Michaelson. $19.95. Oryx Press. 4041 N. Central Ave., Suite #700, Phoenix, AZ 85012. Tel: (602) 265-2651 Fax: (602) 265-6250 E-mail: info@oryxpress.com Web: www.oryxpress.com

How to Write and Present Technical Information by Charles H. Sides. $19.95. Oryx Press, 4041 N. Central Ave., Suite #700, Phoenix, AZ 85012. Tel: (602) 265-2651 Fax: (602) 265-6250 E-mail: info@oryxpress.com Web: www.oryxpress.com

Medical Writing: A Prescription for Clarity: A Self-Help Guide to Clearer Medical English by N.W. Goodman, Dr. Martin B. Edwards and Dr. Andy Black. $19.95. Cambridge University Press.

Health Writer's Handbook by Barbara Gastel, Md. $29.95. Iowa State University Press.

MANUALS

How to Write a Training Manual by John Davis. $55.95 Ashgate Publishing Company.

COMPUTER

How to Write Useable User Documentation by Edmond H. Weiss. $24.95. Oryx Press, 4041 N. Central Ave., Suite #700, Phoenix, AZ 85012. Tel: (602) 265-2651 Fax: (602) 265-6250 E-mail: info@oryxpress.com Web: www.oryxpress.com

How to Write Computer Documentation for Users by Susan Grimm. $44.95. Van Nostrand Reinhold.

BIOGRAPHIES

The Complete Guide to Writing Biographies by Ted Schwarz. Interviewing, writing, marketing and contracting. $19.95. Writer's Digest Books.

Biographers and the Art of Biography by Ulick O'Connor. $28.00. Irish American Book Company.

AUTOBIOGRAPHIES, MEMOIRS, LIFE STORIES

How to Write and Publish Your Family Book by Genealogy Publishing Service. $9.95. Tel: (704) 524-7063.

Family Focused: A Step-by-Step Guide to Writing Your Autobiography by Janice T. Dixon, Ph.D. Mt. Olympus Publishing, P.O. Box 3700, Wendover, NV 89833. Tel: (801) 486-0800; Fax: (801) 486-0849. e-mail: mtoly@wasatch.com

The Times of Our Lives, A Guide to Writing Autobiography and Memoir by Mary Jane Moffat. $8.95. John Daniel and Company, P.O. Box 21922, Santa Barbara, CA 93121. Tel: (805) 962-1780.

How to Write the Story of Your Life by Frank P. Thomas. Unique approach to memoir writing. Resources. $12.99. Betterway Books.

How to Write Your Autobiography by Patricia Ann Case. Unique autobiographical outline. $7.95. Woodbridge Press, P.O. Box 209, Santa Barbara, CA 93102. Tel: (805) 965-7039 Fax: (805) 963-0540 E-mail: woodpress@aol.com Web: www.woodbridgepress.com

How to Publish and Market Your Family History by Carl Boyer III. Researching, writing, systems approach, use of computers and resources. $17.50. Carl Boyer, 3rd, P.O. Box 333, Newhall, CA 91322.

How to Write Your Own Life Story: The Classic Guide for the Nonprofessional Writer by Lois Daniel. A guide with personal experiences told in the first person. $12.95. Chicago Review Press, 814 North Franklin, Chicago, IL 60610-3109.

Writing Articles From the Heart: How to Write and Sell Your Life Experiences by Marjorie Holmes. $16.99. Writer's Digest Books.

Turning Memories into Memoirs: A Handbook for Writing Lifestories by Denis Ledoux. $19.95. Soleil Press.

Writing the Memoir: From Truth to Art by Judith Barrington. $13.95. Eighth Mountain Press.

Your Life as Story: Writing the New Autobiography by Tristine Rainer. $24.95. Tarcher/Putnam.

Living to Tell the Tale: A Guide to Writing Memoir by Jane Taylor McDonnell. $12.95. Penguin.

COOKBOOKS

So You Want to Write a Cookbook! by Judy Rehmel. How to collect recipes, get organized, write, print, self-publish and sell a cookbook. $6.95. Marathon International Publishing, P.O. Box 33008, Louisville, K-Y 40232.

Recipes into Type: A Handbook for Cookbook Writers and Editors by Joan Whitman and Dolores Simon. $27.50. HarperCollins.

The Recipe Writer's Handbook by Barbara Gibbs Ostmann and Jane L. Baker. $34.95. John Wiley & Sons.

TRAVEL

Going Places, The Guide to Travel Guides by Greg Hayes and Joan Wright. A bibliography of 3,000 travel books. $26.95. R.R. Bowker Co., 121 Chanlon Rd., New Providence, NJ 07974. Tel: (888) 269-5372 Web: www.bowker.com

A Guide to Travel Writing & Photography by Ann & Carl Purcell. $22.95. Writer's Digest Books.

How to Make Money From Travel Writing by Curtis Casewitt. Researching, writing, traveling and selling. Resources. $20.00. Peter Smith Publishers.

How to Make a Living as a Travel Writer by Susan Farewell. $10.95. Shooting Star Press.

The Travel Writer's Handbook: How to Write and Sell Your Own Travel Experiences. $15.95. Surrey Books.

Travel Writing by L. Pat O'Neal. $18.99. Writers Digest Books.

Writing About Travel by Morag Campbell. $13.95. A & C Black.

Writing Travel Books and Articles by Richard Cropp, Barbara Braidwood and Susan M. Boyce. $15.95. Self Counsel Press.

Writing Travel Articles That Sell. Three audiotapes by Gordon Burgett. $39.95.

HUMOR

Comedy Writing Secrets by Melvin Helitzer. $16.99. Writer's Digest Books.

Comedy Writing Step by Step by Gene Perret and Carol Burnett. $11.95. Samuel French Trade.

Funny Business: The Craft of Comedy Writing by Sol Saks. $18.95. Lone Eagle Publishing.

The Art of Comedy Writing by Arthur Asa Berger. $29.95. Transaction Publications.

How to Draw & Sell Comic Strips by Alan McKenzie. $19.95. Writer's Digest Books.

How to Draw & Sell Cartoons by Ross Thomson & Bill Hewison. $19.95. Writer's Digest Books.

Cartooning for Kids by Carol Benjamin. $14.89. HarperCollins.

CALENDAR PUBLISHING

Publishing & Marketing Your Calendar: How to Produce and Sell a Profitable Calendar by Calendar Marketing Association. $69.95. 710 Ogden, Suite #600, Naperville, IL 60563. Tel: (630) 369-2406 or (800) 828-8225 E-mail: cma@b-online.com Web: www.calendarmarketplace.com

GREETING CARDS

How to Write & Sell Greeting Cards, Bumper Stickers, T-Shirts & Other Fun Stuff by Molly Wigand. $15.99. Writer's Digest Books.

The Complete Guide to Greeting Card Design & Illustration by Eva Szela. $29.99. Writer's Digest Books.

Writing Comedy Greeting Cards That Sell. Two audiotapes by Gordon Burgett. $34.95. Communications Unlimited, P.O. Box 6405-P, Santa Maria, CA 93456. Tel: (805) 937-8711. Fax: (805) 937-3035.

REGIONAL BOOKS

How to Make Big Profits Publishing City & Regional Books by Marilyn & Tom Ross. $14.95. Communication Creativity, 425 Cedar P.O. Box 909-P, Buena Vista, CO 81211-0909. Tel: (719) 395-8659.

RELIGIOUS BOOKS

Writing for the Religious Market by Marvin E. Ceynar. $3.25 ppd. C.S.S. Publishing Co., 517 South Main Street, PO Box 4503 Lima, OH 45804. Tel: (800) 537-1030. Fax: (419) 228-9184 E-mail: order@csspub.com Web: www.csspub.com

Write for the Religion Market by John A. Moore. $9.95. ETC Publications, 700 E. Vereda Sur, Palm Springs, CA 92262. Tel: (760) 325-5352 Fax: (760) 325-8841.

The Complete Guide to Writing and Selling the Christian Novel by Penelope J. Stokes. $14.99. Writer's Digest Books.

DIRECTORIES

Directory Publishing: A Practical Guide by Russell A. Perkins. $44.95. Cowles/Simba Information Inc. P.O. Box 4234, 11 Riverbend Road, Stamford, CT 06907. Tel: (203) 358-9900; Fax: (203) 358-5824; e-mail: simbainfo@simbanet.com; Web site: http://www.simbanet.com.

Newsletter

The Cowles/Simba Report on Directory Publishing. Cowles/Simba Information Inc. (See above).

FILM/VIDEO/TV/STAGE

For a comprehensive list of books and other resources on screenwriting, see FOD/WEB 638: *Screenwriting: Fiction and Non-fiction* by Gail Kearns

Top Secrets: Screenwriting by Jurgen Wolff and Kerry Cox. $21.95. Lone Eagle. 2337 Roscomare Rd. #9, Los Angeles, CA 90077-1815. Tel: (800) 345-6257 Fax: (310) 479-4969 E-mail: info@loneeagle.com

How to Sell Your Screenplay by Carl Sautter. The real rules of film and television. $14.95. New Chapter Press, 381 Park Avenue South, New York, NY 10016.

Successful Scriptwriting by Jurgen Wolff and Kerry Cox. $16.99. Lone Eagle. 2337 Roscomare Rd. #9, Los Angeles, CA 90077-1815. Tel: (800) 345-6257 Fax: (310) 479-4969 E-mail: info@loneeagle.com

On Screen Writing by Edward Dmytryk. Inside, hands-on scriptwriting. $24.95 ppd. Focal Press 313 Washington Street, Newton, MA 02158-1630. Fax: (617) 928-2640 Web: www.bh.com/fp/

Television & Screen Writing, From Concept to Contract by Richard A. Blum. How-to, examples, markets and resources. $29.95. Focal Press 313 Washington Street, Newton, MA 02158-1630. Fax: (617) 928-2640 Web: www.bh.com/fp/

How to Pitch & Sell Your TV Script by David Silver. Writer's Digest Books.

How to Write for Television by Madeline Maggio. $12.00. Prentice Hall. Imprint of Simon & Shuster. 1 Lake Street, Upper River, NJ 07458. Tel: (201) 236-7000 Web: www.prenhall.com

PHOTO BOOKS

Sell & Re-sell Your Photos by Rohn Engh. What sells, where to sell and pricing. Resources. $14.95. Writer's Digest Books.

Photographer's Market: 2000 Places to Sell Your Photographs edited by Michael Willins. $23.99. Writer's Digest Books.

The Photographer's Guide to Marketing and Self-Promotion by Maria Piscopo. $18.95. Allworth Press. 10 East 23rd Street, New York, New York, 10010. Tel: (212) 777-8395; Fax: (212) 777-8261; e-mail: PUB@allworth.com; Web site: http://www.allworth.com.

Photography for Writers: Using Photography to Increase Your Writing Income. $18.95. Allworth Press. (See above)

JOURNALS

How to Get Published in Business/Professional Journals by Joel J. Shulman. $28.95. Jelmar Publishing Co., PO Box 488, Plainview, NY 11803. Tel: (516) 822-6861.

MAGAZINES

Freelance Writing for Magazines and Newspapers by Marcia Yudkin. A plan for selling your work. Resources. $11.00. HarperCollins Publishers.

Magazine Writing That Sells by Don McKinney. $16.95. Writer's Digest Books.

Complete Guide to Magazine Article Writing by John M. Wilson. $17.99. Writer's Digest Books.

Beginner's Guide to Writing & Selling Quality Features by Charlotte Digregorio. A simple course in freelancing for newspapers and magazines. $12.95. Civetta Press, P.O. Box 1043-P, Portland, OR 97207-1043. Tel: (503) 228-6649.

NEWSLETTERS, NEWSPAPERS

Publishing Newsletters by Howard Penn Hudson. 224 pgs., $39.95. H&M Publishing, 44 West Market Street, P.O. Box 311, Rhinebeck, N.Y. 12572 Tel: (800) 572-3451; Fax: (914) 876-2561; e-mail: HPHudson@aol.com

The Newsletter Handbook; How to Produce a Successful Newsletter by Wesley Dorsheimer. 194 Pages, $14.95. Hippocrene Books. Tel: (201) 568-5194; Tel: (201) 894-5406.

Newsletter Sourcebook by Mark Beach. 137 pgs., $29.95. Writer's Digest Books.

Editing Your Newsletter by Mark Beach. $22.95. Writer's Digest Books.

Success in Newsletter Publishing; A Practical Guide by Frederick D. Goss. $39.50. Newsletter. Association, 1401 Wilson Blvd., #403, Arlington, VA 22209. Tel: (800) 356-9302.

How to Do Leaflets, Newletters & Newspapers by Nancy Brigham. $14.95. Writer's Digest Books.

Also contact Newsletter on Newsletters, Howard Penn Hudson, P.O. Box 311, Rhinebeck, NY 12572. Tel: :(800) 572-3451 or (914) 876-2081.

CONTRACTING/LEGAL

Business Guide to Copyright Law by Woody Young. Complete explanations with forms. $14.95. Joy Publishing (Para Publishing).

The Copyright Permission and Libel Handbook by Lloyd J. Jassin and Steven C. Schechter. $14.95. John Wiley & Sons.

Business and Legal Forms for Authors & Self-Publishers by Tad Crawford. Has actual tear-out forms and contracts. $19.95. Allworth Press. (Para Publishing).

Business and Legal Forms for Graphic Designers by Tad Crawford. $22.95. Writer's Digest Books.

Publishing Agreements by Charles Clark. Sample contracts with explanations. International. $29.95. New Amsterdam Books. (Para Publishing).

SELLING INFORMATION

Writer's Market: 4000 Places to Sell What You Write edited by Kristen Holm. $27.99. Writer's Digest Books.

How to Make a Whole Lot More than $1,000,000 Writing, Commissioning, Publishing and Selling "How-To" Information by Jeffrey Lant. $39.95. (Para Publishing.)

A Beginner's Guide to Getting Published by Kirk Polking. $11.95. Writer's Digest Books.

The Writer's Handbook. How and where to sell magazine articles, poetry, greeting card verses, fillers, scripts and book manuscripts. An anthology of helpful chapters with a lengthy directory of resources. $30.70 ppd. The Writer, 120 Boylston Street, Boston, MA 02116. Tel: (617) 423-3157 or (888) 273-8214 Fax: (617) 423-2168 E-mail: writer@user1.channel1.com Web: www.channel1.com/thewriter/

Money for Writer$ edited by Billot. Includes grants, awards, prizes, contests, scholarships, retreats, conferences and Internet information. $19.95. Henry Holt.

The Writer's Resource Handbook by Daniel Grant. Includes career assistance, grants and awards, writers-in-residence programs, creative writing programs, legal and accounting services and insurance. $19.95. Allworth Press.

Getting Published, The Acquisition Process at University Presses by Paul Parsons. $33.00. The University of Tennessee Press, 293 Communications Building, Knoxville, TN 37996-0325. Fax: (423) 974-3724 E-mail: jsiler@utk.edu Web: www.lib.utk.edu/utkgophers/utpress

PUBLISHING

The Self-Publishing Manual, How to Write, Print & Sell Your Own Book by Dan Poynter. The complete manual on book production, marketing and distribution. Eleventh revised edition, 464 pages. $19.95. Para Publishing. Call 1(800) PARAPUB. See http://www.ParaPublishing.com

A Beginner's Guide to Self-Publishing by Kathleen Gilbert. 24 pages. $4.50 ppd. Violetta Books, P.O. Box 15151, Springfield, NH 01105.

Self-Publishing to Niche Markets by Gordon Burgett. $14.95. Communications Unlimited. (Para Publishing).

How to Get Happily Published by Judith Appelbaum. How to write, find a publisher or locate an agent. $11.95. Harper & Row. (Para Publishing).

Mastering the Business of Writing: A Leading Literary Agent Reveals the Secrets of Success by Richard Curtis. $18.95. Allworth Press. 10 East 23rd Street, New York, New York, 10010. Tel: (212) 777-8395; Fax: (212) 777-8261; e-mail: PUB@allworth.com; Web site: http://www.allworth.com.

The Shortest Distance Between You and a Published Book: 20 Steps to Success by Susan Page. $13.00. Broadway Books.

The Portable Writers' Conference: Your Guide to Getting and Staying Published edited by Stephen Blake Mettee. Great advice from over 45 editors, agents & authors. $19.95. Quill Driver Books/Word Dancer Press, Inc., 950 N. Van Ness, P.O. Box 4638, Fresno, CA 93744. Tel: (800) 497-4909.

The Young Author's Do-It-Yourself Book: How to Write, Illustrate & Produce Your Own Book by Donna Guthrie, et. al. $15.40. Millbrook Press, 2 Old New Milford Road, Brookfield, CT 06804. Web: www.neca.com/mall/millbrook

BOOK PROPOSALS

How to Write a Book Proposal by Michael Larsen. Examples and resources to help you approach a publisher or agent.$14.99. Writer's Digest Books.

Nonfiction Book Proposals Anybody Can Write: How to Get a Contract & Advance Before You Write Your Book by Elizabeth Lyon. $14.95. Blue Heron Publishing, 24450 NW Hansen Rd, Hillsboro, OR 97124.

Books listed with Para Publishing in parenthesis are available from Para Publishing

Para Publishing
PO Box 8206-890
Santa Barbara, CA 93118-8206 USA
Tel: (805) 968-7277
Fax: (805) 968-1379

AUDIOTAPES ON WRITING

Audiotapes from A Cappela Publishing, P.O. Box 3691, Sarasota, FL 34234; Tel/Fax: (941) 361-3481; e-mail: acappub@aol.com; Web site: http://www. acappela.com

Why Your Book Doesn't Work (1 hour)
Openings That Hook Readers (1 hour)
Choosing Your Voice (1 hour)
Bringing Your Characters to Life (1 hour)
Plots That Intrigue (1 hour)
Writing Your Own Life Story (4 hours; not sold separately)

Prices: Single tape — $15.00; Any two tapes — $27.00; Any four tapes — $45.00

Bird by Bird: Some Instructions on Writing and Life by Anne Lamott. Step-by-step pointers on to live a writer's life. An inspirational guide. 2 cassettes. $17.95. Audio Partners Publishing.

OTHER RESOURCES

BROCHURES ON BOOKS of interest to writers and publishers are available from:

Para Publishing, P.O. Box 8206-890, Santa Barbara, CA 93118-8206. Tel: (800) PARAPUB.

R.R. Bowker Co., 121 Chanlon Rd., New Providence, NJ 07974. Tel: (888) 269-5372 Web: www.bowker.com

Dustbooks, P.O. Box 100 Paradise, CA 95967. Tel: (800) 477-6110 Fax: (530) 877-0222 E-mail: dustbooks@telis.org Web: www.dustbooks.com

Gale Research Co., Book Tower, Detroit, MI 48226.

The Writer, 120 Boylston Street, Boston, MA 02116. Tel: (617) 423-3157 or (888) 273-8214 Fax: (617) 423-2168 E-mail: writer@user1. channel1.com Web: www.channel1.com/thewriter/

Writer's Digest Books, 1507 Dana Avenue, Cincinnati, OH 45207.

REFERENCE BOOKS AND DIRECTORIES may be used and previewed at the Reference Desk in your local public library. Write the publishers for ordering details.

From R.R. Bowker Co., 121 Chanlon Rd., New Providence, NJ 07974. Tel: (888) 269-5372 Web: www.bowker.com

Literary Market Place. Very important. Lists agents, artists, associations, book clubs, reviewers, exporters, magazines, newspapers, news services, radio & TV, and many other services. Annual.

International Literary Market Place. Lists publishers, agents, suppliers, etc. in 160 countries outside the U.S. and Canada.

Books in Print. Lists all the books currently available by subject, title, and author. Annual

Subject Guide to Forthcoming Books. A preview of *Books in Print.*

From Dustbooks, P.O. Box 100 Paradise, CA 95967. Tel: (800) 477-6110 Fax: (530) 877-0222 E-mail: dustbooks@telis.org Web: www.dustbooks.com

> *International Directory of Little Magazines and Small Presses*
> *Small Press Record of Books in Print*
> *Directory of Small Press/Magazine Editors & Publishers*
> *Directory of Poetry Publishers*

MAGAZINES AND NEWSLETTERS FOR AUTHORS. Write for a sample copy and current subscription rates.

Small Press Review, P.O. Box 100 Paradise, CA 95967. Tel: (800) 477-6110 Fax: (530) 877-0222 E-mail: dustbooks@telis.org Web: www.dustbooks.com

Writer's Digest, 1507 Dana Avenue, Cincinnati, OH 45207.

The Writer, 120 Boylston Street, Boston, MA 02116. Tel: (617) 423-3157 or (888) 273-8214 Fax: (617) 423-2168 E-mail: writer@user1.channel1. com Web: www.channel1.com/thewriter/

Writer's Journal, P.O. Box 25376, Saint Paul, MN 55125. Tel: (612) 730-4280.

PAMPHLETS AND REPORTS OF INTEREST TO AUTHORS. Write for latest prices.

P.E.N. American Center, 568 Broadway, Suite #401, New York, NY 10012. Tel: (212) 334-1660 Fax: (212) 334-2181 E-mail: pen@echony.com Web: www.pen.org

> *Grants and Awards Available to American Writers*

National Endowment for the Arts, Literature Program, 2401 E Street NW, Washington, DC 20506. Assistance, fellowships and residences for writers.

Poets & Writers, 72 Spring Street, New York, NY 10012. Tel: (212) 226-3586 or (800) 666-2268 Fax: (212) 226-3963 E-mail: infocenter@pwonline.com or pwsubs@aol.com Web: www.pw.org

> *A Writer's Guide to Copyright*
> *Writers Conferences: An Annual Guide to Literary Conferences*

Writer's Digest Books, 1507 Dana Avenue, Cincinnati, OH 45207.

> *Getting Started in Writing*
> *Jobs & Opportunities for Writers*
> *Should You Pay to Have it Published?*

WRITERS CONFERENCES

Maui Writers' Conference (Labor Day weekend), P.O. Box 1118, Kihea, HI 96753. Tel: (808) 879-0061; Fax: (808) 879-6233; e-mail: writers@maui.net; Web site: http://www.mauiwriters.com

Santa Barbara Writers' Conference (third week of June), P.O. Box 304, Carpinteria, CA 93014. Tel: (805) 684-2250.

The William Saroyan Writers Conference (late March), Writer's International Network, P.O. Box 5331, Fresno, CA 93755. Tel: (209) 224-2516. Presented in Association with *Publishers Weekly*.

Each year, *Writer's Digest* puts out a complete guide to Writers' Conferences, Seminars and Workshops. Write or call for more information. *Writer's Digest*, 1507 Dana Avenue, Cincinnati, OH 45207. Tel: (513) 531-2222; e-mail: writersdigest@fwpubs.com

PROFESSIONAL ORGANIZATIONS. Write for an application and inquire about benefits and dues. Many associations publish a magazine or newsletter. For a more complete list, see *Writer's Market*.

Mystery Writers of America, 17 E. 47th Street, 6th Floor, New York, NY 10017. Tel: (212) 888-8171 Fax: (212) 888-8107 Web: www.mysterywriters. org/

Sisters in Crime, P.O. Box 442124, Lawrence, KS 66044. Tel: (913) 842-1325.

Western Writers of America, 256 Braeburst Circle, Marble Falls, TX 78654. Tel: (615) 791-1444; Web site: http://www.imt.net/~gedison/wwa/html

National Writers Union, 113 University Place, 6th Floor, New York, NY 10003. Tel: (212) 254-0279 Fax: (212) 254-0673 E-mail: nwu@wu.org Web: www.nwu.org/nwu

Academy of American Poets, 584 E. Broadway, New York, N.Y. 10012. Tel: (212) 247-0343; Fax: (212) 274-9427; Web site: http://www.tmn. com/Artswire/poets/page.html

Poets & Writers, 72 Spring Street, New York, NY 10012. Tel: (212) 226-3586 or (800) 666-2268 Fax: (212) 226-3963 E-mail: infocenter@pwonline.com or pwsubs@aol.com Web: www.pw.org

PEN American Center, 568 Broadway, Suite #401, New York, NY 10012. Tel: (212) 334-1660 Fax: (212) 334-2181 E-mail: pen@echony.com Web: www.pen.org

Writer's Guild of America, East Chapter: 555 West 57th Street, New York, NY 10019. Tel: (212) 767-7800 West Chapter: 7000 West Third Street, Los Angeles, CA 90048. Registration Tel: (213) 782-4540 Web: www.wga.org

Authors League of America, 234 West 44th Street, New York, NY 10036. Tel: (212) 564-8350.

American Society of Journalists & Authors, 1501 Broadway, Suite #302, New York, NY 10036. Tel: (212) 997-0947 Fax: (212) 768-7414 E-mail: asja@compuserve.com Web: www.asja.com

National Association of Science Writers, P.O. Box 294, Greenlawn, NY 11740. Tel: (516) 757-5664 Fax: (516) 757-0069 Web: www.nasw.org

Outdoor Writers Association of America, 2155 E. Cato Ave., State College, PA 16801. Tel: (814) 234-1011 Fax: (814) 234-9692 E-mail: eking4owaa @compuserve.com

Society for Technical Communication, 901 N. Stuart, Suite #904, Arlington, VA 22203. Tel: (703) 522-4114 Fax: (703) 522-2075 Web: www.stc-va.org

Eastern Ski Writers, 7 Lattimer Street, Marblehead, MA 01945-2427. Tel: (781) 639-3792.

Society of American Travel Writers, 4101 Lake Boone Trail, Suite #201, Raleigh, NC 27607. Tel: (919) 787-5181 Fax: (919) 787-4916 Web: www.writersmarketplace.com

American Medical Writers Association, 9650 Rockville Pike, Bethesda, MD 20814-3928. Tel: (301) 493-0003 Fax: (301) 493-6384 E-mail: amwa@amwa.org Web: www.amwa.org

Garden Writers Association of America, 10210 Leatherleaf Court, Manassas, VA 20111-4245. Tel: (703) 257-1032.

Horror Writers Association, P.O. Box 423, Oak Forest, IL 60452. E-mail: hwa@horror.org; Web site: http://www.horror.org/hwa/

Romance Writers of America, 13700 Veterans Memorial Drive, Suite #315, Houston, TX 77014-1023. Tel: (281) 440-6885 Fax: (281) 440-7510 Web: www.rwanational.com

Association of Authors Representatives, 10 Astor Place, New York, NY 10003-6935. Tel: (212) 353-3709.

Western Writers of America, James Crutchfield, 1012 Fair Street, Franklin, TN 37064. Web site: http://www.imt.net/~gedison/wwahome.html

National Writers Association, 1450 South Havana, Suite #424, Aurora, CO 80012. Tel: (303) 751-8593 Fax: (303) 751-8593 E-mail: Sandywriter @aol.com

International Association of Business Communicators, One Hallidie Plaza, Suite #600, San Francisco, CA 94102. Tel: (415) 433-3400 Fax: (415) 362-8762 E-mail: service-center@iabc.com Web: www.iabc.com

Canadian Authors Association, 27 Doxsee Ave., N. Cambellford, Ontario, K0L 1L0, Canada. Tel: (705) 653-0323 Fax: (705) 653-0593 E-mail: canauth@redden.on.ca Web: www.canauthors.org/national.html

Periodical Writers Association, 54 Wolfeley Street, Suite #203, TOR M5T 1A5, Canada. Tel: (416) 504-1645 Fax: (416) 703-0059 E-mail: pwac@web.net Web: www.web.net/~pwac

Education Writers Association, 1331 H St. NW, Suite 302, Washington, DC 20005. Tel: (202) 637-9700; Fax: (202) 637-9707; e-mail: ewaoffice@aol.com

WEB SITES OF INTEREST TO WRITERS

A Cappela Publishing
Lectures, Writing Seminars, Books & Tapes
http://www.acappela.com

Allworth Press
Books for the Creative Professional
http://www.allworth.com

Amazon.com
An online bookstore that has many reviews of the books it sells.
http://www.Amazon.com

Big Yellow Pages
http://www.bigyellow.com

Bookwire (links to many author websites)
http://www.bookwire.com

Book Zone
http://www.bookzone.com

Children's Writing Resource Center
http://www.write4kids.com/index.html

Dictionary Links
http://www.yahoo.com/reference/dictionaries/

Inkspot Writer's Forum
http://www.inkspot.com

Media Research Center
http://www.mediaresearch.org

My Virtual Reference Desk
http://www.refdesk.com/facts.html

Para Publishing
http://www.ParaPublishing.com

The Small Publishers, Artists and Writers Network
http://www.spawn.org

Writers Guild of America
http://www.wga.org/

Writer's Resources
http://www.interlog.com/books.html

INDEX

How to Order FOD/Web Documents

Throughout this book we make reference to other Documents for more information. They may be retrieved from our Fax-On-Demand system or from our web site.

Fax-On-Demand: Call (805) 968-8947 from your fax machine, follow the voice prompts and request Documents 109 and 601 which are free menus of documents. The menus will tell you how to retrieve the Documents mentioned in this book as well as other (new) reports.

Web site: http://www.parapublishing.com/books/para/p

Most Documents are Free. Instant Reports in the 6XX series are modestly priced.

The world is before you, and you need not take it or leave it as it was when you came in. — James Baldwin

IS THERE AN AUTHOR IN YOUR LIFE?

I know the following people have a book inside them and I want to help.
Please send them a FREE writing/publishing information kit.

Name: _____

Address: _____

City: _____ State: _____ Zip: _____

Name: _____

Address: _____

City: _____ State: _____ Zip: _____

Name: _____

Address: _____

City: _____ State: _____ Zip: _____

Name: _____

Address: _____

City: _____ State: _____ Zip: _____

Mail this form to Para Publishing, P O Box 8206-P, Santa Barbara, CA
93118-8206

COLOPHON

This book was completely produced with computerized equipment. The authors used computers for gathering and filing information as well as for writing, editing and even setting the type. This book is an example of typesetting with a computer.

PRODUCTION NOTES
 Composition
   Input: The 5th Edition of *Is There A Book Inside You?* was designed using QuarkXPress
   Output: Postscript files were output to film by McNaughton & Gunn using a Linotronic 530 at 2540 lpi resolution
   Text: Utopia
   Headlines: Poppl-Laudatio
   Quotes: Utopia Italic
 Book Design and Production:
   Cirrus Design, Santa Barbara, CA
 Cover art: Robert Howard
 Paper:
   Text, 60-pound white offset book
   Cover, 10 pt. C1S white
 Ink:
   Text, standard black
   Cover, four colors with film lamination
 Printing:
   Offset lithography, McNaughton & Gunn
   Ann Arbor, Michigan
 Binding:
   Perfect (adhesive)

Quick Order Form

Fax orders: (805) 968-1379. Send this form.

Telephone orders: Call 1(800) PARAPUB toll free, (727-2782). Have your credit card ready.

E-mail orders: orders@ParaPublishing.com.

Postal orders: Para Publishing, Dan Poynter, PO Box 8206-146, Santa Barbara, CA 93118-8206. USA. Telephone: (805) 968-7277

Please send the following Books, Discs or Reports. I understand that I may return any of them for a full refund—for any reason, no questions asked.

_____

_____

_____

Please send more FREE information on:

☐ Other books, ☐ Speaking/Seminars, ☐ Mailing lists, ☐ Consulting

Name: _____

Address: _____

City: _____ State: _____ Zip: _____ – _____

Telephone: _____

E-mail address: _____

Sales tax: Please add 7.75% for products shipped to California addresses.

Shipping by air:

US: $4 for the first book or disk and $2.00 for each additional product.
International: $9 for 1st book or disk: $5 for each additional product (estimate).

Payment: ☐ Cheque, ☐ Credit card:

☐ Visa, ☐ MasterCard, ☐ Optima, ☐ AMEX, ☐ Discover

Card number: _____

Name on card: _____ Exp. date: _____ /_____